To Mike
Have a lovely Christmas

Liz + Leighton
x x x

TALES OF A
Coarse Angler

David Plummer

The Oxford Illustrated Press

ISBN 0 946609 53 5

Published by:
The Oxford Illustrated Press Limited, Haynes
Publishing Group, Sparkford, Nr Yeovil, Somerset
BA22 7JJ, England.

Haynes Publications Inc., 861 Lawrence Drive,
Newbury Park, California 91320, USA.

Printed in England by:
J.H. Haynes and Co. Limited, Sparkford, Nr. Yeovil,
Somerset.

British Library Cataloguing in Publication Data:
Plummer, David
  Tales of a course angler.
  1. Great Britain. Coarse fish. Angling –
  Personal observations
  I. Title
  799.1'1
  ISBN 0-946609-53-5

Library of Congress Catalog Card Number
  87-83274

Line illustrations by Chris Turnbull

Acknowledgements

First I must thank Vic Bellars for all the time and effort
he has devoted to helping me write this book. Not least
his skill in being able to talk to and question me for
hours on end and by so doing, draw out the full richness
of my angling experiences. It would have been difficult
to have written the book without his encouragement.

Mention must be given to those fine anglers, Tony
Miles, Trefor West, Andy Barker, Clive Diedrich,
Richard Furlong and Derrick Amies and many more.

All have unstintingly passed on their hard-won
knowledge without which I could not have hoped to
enjoy the success as an angler that it has been my good
fortune to enjoy.

I would like to think that all of them have perhaps
learnt just a little from me in return.

And last but not least, I would like to acknowledge
my debt to my father who introduced me to the sport all
those years ago.

Dedication

To my wife Linda who has shared my triumphs and
disappointments, who was full of encouragement when I
gave up my career in order to open a fishing tackle shop
and who has been most tolerant and understanding of
my deep love of angling. If in the future I can count on
such support I shall be a truly happy man.

Contents

Foreword

Every generation produces a handful of truly outstanding anglers, men who are not merely good or very good at fishing, but men who possess that certain extra indefinable quality that sets them apart from the rest. Such individuals appear to possess an almost telepathic understanding of fish, a divine gift for angling that ensures that, almost effortlessly it often appears, they catch more and bigger fish than those around them, and more often.

Without a shadow of a doubt, just such a man is Dave Plummer, the author of this book. Dave is a tremendously gifted and highly successful all rounder, with a breathtaking big fish list, and yet a man who is renowned for his willingness to help others. Dave and I have been close friends for many years, and I record here my gratitude for all the assistance he has given me during my frequent trips to Norfolk.

Without question, Dave Plummer has owed the angling world a book for a long time, for he has so much to share. This book provides a fascinating insight into his fishing, told as it is around many of the different waters he has tackled over the years. It is all here, from the wild unpredictability of Lomond to the heart-stopping thrill of a surging run at Cassien. I count myself privileged to have shared some of the experiences written about in this book: I too have enjoyed chasing those magnificent Wensum barbel and chub; I too have caught my breath as my pike float slides away on the Thurne, and together Dave and I first experienced the serenity of Redmire pool.

Within these pages, therefore, is captured a lifetime's experience of fish and fishing, written by a man whose dedication to, and enthusiasm for, the sport is infectious. Although not deliberately intended to be an instructional work, it contains a wealth of knowledge imparted in an eminently readable and enjoyable style.

Undeniably, Dave Plummer is a giant in the big fish scene of today, and, by this token, his book is an important contribution to modern angling literature. It will certainly command a prominent position on my bookshelf.

TONY MILES
DECEMBER 1987

4

On the Bonnie Bonnie Banks . . .

Ten thousand years ago, a mile-deep mantle of ice that covered most of the British Isles, began to thaw. On four separate occasions Britain had endured an Ice Age, these glacial epochs occurring every 150 million years. The forces exerted by the infinitesimally slow but inexorable movement of a glacier are immense and the Scottish glens are testimony to the power of a mile-deep icefield grinding to powder rock as hard as granite, and scouring out wide troughs through the hills. As the ice melted, lakes formed in these gouged out valleys and so Loch Lomond was formed, to remain to this day, the largest stretch of freshwater in these islands, excluding Eire; a loch nestling in the mountainous highlands, ever replenished by rain and melting snow from the rivers draining the hillsides.

When I first saw Lomond in 1966 I was unprepared for her size and the rugged grandeur and breathtaking beauty of her surrounding terrain. As a Yorkshireman I was at home in wild moorland country, but the highlands with their snow-clad mountain peaks and steep slopes patterned in subtle tones of dark green, brown and blue-black were awe inspiring. The cloud shadows as they raced across the hills and loch constantly changed the tonal values so that a sombre stand of woodland lost in shadow would become suddenly transformed into a riot of yellow and green. Shafts of sunlight were caught and held by the ripples on the loch, so for a few moments the surface flashed and sparkled as though strewn with diamonds.

Until then I had been used to fishing in far smaller waters, but even a large reservoir seemed a puddle in comparison to the immensity of Lomond. This vast sweep of water, akin to an inland sea, was studded with wooded islands and dangerous rocky outcrops which menacingly parted the foam-flecked surface. I stood for many minutes trying to take in the enormity of the loch and wondering how best to fish it.

Loch Lomond is 23 miles in length and some 6 miles wide by its southern shore. The chart shows most of the loch to be 50 to 100 feet deep though it is 600 feet deep in one spot—not a water to trifle with. In a gale the surface can be whipped into high waves capable of overwhelming an

open boat, waves that would not disgrace an angry ocean.

Why Loch Lomond lured me so far from home and away from the more gentle waters of Yorkshire was because like every other angler I dreamt of catching an enormous fish and I had read of the great pike reputed to exist in Lomond: of Tommy Morgan's 47 lb 11 oz pike caught in 1945 and of a huge dead pike found in 1934 at the mouth of the river Endrick that flows into the loch just south of Balmaha. That fish was never weighed, but the great head was preserved, and many years later, the late and legendary angler Richard Walker was able to handle this slab of a head, examine it minutely, photograph it and after careful deliberation announce that in its prime it could have weighed 70 lb. If that is hardly credible, then in 1862 a John Norton and Patrick Sheeney trolling in Lough Derg (another huge water), caught a goliath of a fish of $92^{1}/_{2}$ lb. This is in fact the world record pike, but although many discredit this fish as a flight of fancy, Fred Buller, the authority on the subject is convinced that the reports were accurate, for not only was that great fish weighed but there were many witnesses to confirm it.

Vast waters, provided that there are ample stocks of fish for pike to prey on are therefore known to produce pike of exceptional size. Indeed, similar big waters in Europe harbour huge pike of 60 lb, and in North America a similar species, the Musky, are known to grow as large. For all these reasons I was therefore convinced that enormous pike lurked in Lomond's 18,000 acres and I was determined to fish the loch as often as possible.   In the 1950s, fishermen's attitude to their sport began to change. Previously it had always been considered a matter of luck if a big fish was caught, but now a new generation of anglers were convinced that large fish could be caught by design rather than by accident. New tackle capable of handling big fish (in particular specialist rods, due to the influence of Richard Walker) were becoming available as was monofilament line. Individual anglers teamed up with others so that expertise and experience could be shared. These groups of mainly young anglers were termed 'Specimen Groups', for they were interested in catching large fish—the specimens. Soon the angling press began to publish reports of large fish being caught by specimen anglers and the big fish scene had arrived.

The South Yorkshire Specimen Group was formed and not long after I was able to join their ranks. Some of us were keen pike anglers and we very quickly considered the possibility of searching out waters that might hold large pike. Irish pike are legendary, but much as we would have liked to fish her huge loughs, time and expense precluded this, so we settled for

Scotland and Loch Lomond seemed an obvious choice. We planned a campaign enthusiastically designed to culminate in the capture of one of the Lomond giants.

We spent many an evening arguing and planning, and as each pint of beer was consumed our confidence grew. Twenty-three miles of water takes some getting to know—a lifetime—but such difficulties, if not dismissed, were made light of. We were also confident that the tackle we possessed was capable of coping with any pike that swam. But dedication, the greatest expertise and the most advanced fishing tackle cannot ensure that some great fish will grace the landing net, though these may shorten the odds a little. Luck and fate still play their part as has been proved time and time again when a beginner or the very inexperienced has caught the fish of a lifetime.

It seemed to me foolish to start fishing Lomond without at least a modicum of knowledge of the habits and location of the pike in this vast expanse of water, so I corresponded with both Richard Walker and Fred Buller who had fished the loch, and concentrated for a time in the area where Tommy Morgan's fine pike had been caught. Some anglers are jealous of their hard-won secrets, but all those I contacted went out of their way to give me as much help as possible and I shall remain greatly indebted to them for their kindness. Another specimen group based in Norwich, the Norfolk Grebes had already explored part of the loch in the Balmaha region. Brian Cannel one of the group also freely told me all he knew, as did others.

Once I began to fish Lomond I could draw on local knowledge; the boat hire proprietors offered sound advice as did the Scots anglers themselves even though few have bothered to fish specifically for them. For generations the Scots have preferred to fish for salmon, sea trout and the native brown trout, and pike, however large, were considered vermin— there are still dyed-in-the-wool anglers today who consider the only good pike is a dead one. Such an attitude ignores the fact that predation maintains nature's precarious balance. A species immune from predation will suffer a population explosion that will exhaust its food supply causing individuals to become stunted in growth and prone to disease through overcrowding. In freshwater the pike is at the peak of the ecological pyramid, a successful predator essential for the well-being of our indigenous fish stocks.

Silvery salmon and seatrout enter Loch Lomond via the river Leven which empties into the loch at its southern end. Being so close to the populous conurbation of Glasgow the Leven is heavily netted and poached. Yet in spite of this heavy toll, taken both legally and illegally, a number of these game fish enter the loch in order to run through to their spawning redds in the rivers that feed the loch. The routes these migratory fish take year after year are well known. So when the runs are taking place the local anglers troll artificial lures behind a moving boat. As comparatively few salmon and seatrout reach the loch these anglers troll for hour after hour concentrating on the paths that countless generations of game fish have habitually followed. The lures that these anglers use imitate a small fish, fluttering, wobbling and shining as they are pulled through the water. They attract salmon and sea trout but also of course the predatory pike. By talking to the trollers I soon discovered specific areas where pike were often caught on lures, for they too were well aware of the routes taken by the game fish, and each year would concentrate along the paths, for the same reasons as the anglers. When we saw a number of trolling boats working we fished for pike nearby, almost certain that some would be in the vicinity.

In late May of 1966 Albert Ibbotson (a member of our group) visited Ardlui which is situated at the northernmost extremity of the loch. I had planned to follow on and after the long lonely drive north I saw Loch Lomond for the first time. Ardlui near where the river Falloch enters the loch is hardly a village. There is a hotel, a caravan site boasting a small shop and a tiny railway station on the line to Callender and far off Fort William. Nearby odd farm buildings sheltered on the lower slope of the hills by the side of the loch. After the stuffiness of the van and the decidedly fishy aroma of my well-used fishing tackle, it was a relief to take great breaths of the pure air. Great expanses of water such as that spread out before my gaze affect the quality of the atmosphere; the air was heady, strong and ozonic.

I hurried to contact Albert at our hired caravan. I was bursting with questions but he had little to report, certainly no tales of great fish. But undismayed we planned the next day's fishing for I was itching to get afloat on what we both believed to be an angler's Mecca. Boats could be obtained from the small boatyard run by Eric Wallace, and next morning we selected a stout 12-foot rowing boat which to our inexperienced eyes seemed excellent. To save time and the exertion of long spells of rowing as we moved from one part of the loch to another we had brought along an outboard motor. We felt that no area of the loch, however remote, was beyond our reach.

Without experience of huge expanses of water we were unprepared for the heavy swell often topped by curling wave crests that could transform a placid calm into a turmoil of heaving water in a matter of minutes. Because we had chosen to fish the northernmost end of the loch the Fates decided that an increasing southerly wind would blow for the remainder of our stay. Lomond is narrow for many miles to the south of Ardlui and as it is hemmed in either side by mountains reaching skyward for two thousand feet, and on the western shore by one peak even higher, any wind from the south is funnelled down the loch, so creating a swell more appropriate to the open sea.

Dismayed, we watched the steady increase in wind strength and realised that it would be foolhardy to launch our cockleshell of a boat, so we retired to the caravan and pored over the chart searching for some area sheltered from the wind, and even more important, that we could reach without having to cross rough waters. Luckily there was an inlet close by that seemed to offer a haven.

Naturally we had no idea if pike would be present, but we had no option but to fish there since it was the only safe place. Loading the gear aboard we set off on our reconnaissance, reached the mouth of the inlet without incident and motored into what appeared to be shallow water, no more than five or six feet deep. The water was clear and we could see the bottom which was covered in thick weed like a flooded hay meadow. Here and there boulders littered the loch bed as did trees and branches that had been transported down the river that entered the inlet. Uprooted by the winter torrents these waterlogged tree trunks had settled to form an underwater jungle of intertwined and twisted branches. Rocky outcrops protruded from the surface as miniature islands. In such a snag-ridden place it would be difficult to fish effectively. In fact the only feasible way to fish at all would be to spin artificial lures or wobble deadbaits; we settled on the latter method.

Wobbling can best be described as casting, then slowly retrieving a dead fish such as a red-finned roach, a spotted trout, a silver herring or some similar sized fish. The fish is mounted on two treble hooks some $2^{1}/2$ inches apart fixed to a thin but strong, flexible multi-strand wire trace. Wire is absolutely essential for catching pike for the fish's shovel-shaped mouth is armed with needle-sharp teeth that can slice through monofilament fishing line however strong. This wire trace some eighteen inches long is joined to the reel line by a small revolving swivel. One arm of the upper treble holds the bait firmly by being passed through both lips,

9

the other treble is fixed in the bait's flank, level with, or just behind, the dorsal fin.

We were soon casting and wobbling, trying by means of jerking the rod tip and varying the speed of retrieve to make the baits dart, sink, rise and flutter; to make then appear alive and also to give the appearance of a sick or wounded fish, an easy meal for any marauding pike. Naturally we chose to use our normal pike tackle that had proved so efficient in English waters; 10-lb line and a 20-lb wire trace. We were very quickly disillusioned. There were pike in the inlet, in fact pike in plenty. They took kindly to the wobbled baits and we hooked a number of them, but sad to relate those wild fish parted our lines like weak cotton as they powered off in uncontrollable runs, and often as not, buried themselves in the bottom weed or found sanctuary in the litter of tree branches. Sometimes the line scraped the rocky boulders with disastrous results, snapping as easily as a gossamer thread. Used as we both were to playing sizeable pike we could hardly credit the speed and power of these loch fish, so unlike their southern counterparts that they might have been a different species. These pike literally charged along on the surface—I had read graphic descriptions of tail-walking pike, now I was seeing it for myself. Interspersed with this athleticism these fish leapt entirely clear of the water crashing back in a smother of foam and cascading water droplets. If after such a performance they were still hooked they set off like fast-running torpedoes. If it was exhilarating, it was also nerve shattering and it soon became apparent that our tackle was not man enough for the job. Short of line and short of baits we had to admit defeat, and reluctantly we started the outboard and sped back to the landing stage. Realising that we were most inadequately equipped for catching loch pike, we made a few enquiries and we were able to locate and purchase some much heavier line of 18-lb breaking strain. We also increased the length of the wire traces in an attempt to prevent the line being frayed to tatters as it rasped against the granite boulders.

So armed, we returned to the inlet the following day. Certainly it was still the only place we could fish with safety; that pernicious southerly wind seemed to be blowing with increased ferocity. We cast our baits and worked them along those dense weedbeds that grew to the surface, wobbling them enticingly by the sun-bleached trunks of dead trees and close by the forests of sunken branches. The clarity of the water was unbelievable—clear as crystal glass—and we could see the baits gyrating and flashing silver. Once I was mesmerised as four or five pike, appearing like fleeting green-blue shadows converged on my bait. In all the years I have fished, both before and since I have never seen the like and my memory remains vividly clear, clear as Lomond's translucent depths.

The heavier line and longer traces soon proved their worth. Several fish up to 10 lb were hooked, played and boated, but the highlight of that memorable day was the 16½-lb fish that fought so hard that it strained the new strong line close to breaking point. A 16-lb fish is called in angling parlance 'a good double', a 'double' being any fish weighing between 10 lb and 20 lb. Albert and I gazed at this, our first sizeable loch pike, in admiration. Up to that time we had caught many pike of similar size and even larger. We were used to English lake pike, broad of head and of ample girth that could bear comparison with the rotundity of a well fed politician. But this glorious specimen was much longer than its southern cousins, it was lean and lithe like a long-distance athlete, solid muscle from snout to tail. No doubt due to its clear water environment its markings were spectacular: the green back contrasting with richly barred flanks overlaid with a dapple of yellow spots that merged into a pale creamy underside. The fins were a strong brown-orange and appeared to be larger than the fins on English pike. But perhaps most impressive of all, and no doubt accounting for its amazing speed and acceleration, was the immense spread of its tail. A Lomond pike is built for speed and stamina; this great tail, set just behind the sail-like anal and dorsal fins, provides the driving power. Together, these three fins, sinuously thrusting in unison, can generate great force that propels the superbly streamlined body forward in a burst of speed; speed from a standing start so that in a split second the fish is surging forward at maximum pace. The long lean Lomond pike have evolved in order to exploit their particular environment to the full.

In huge expanses of water the species that pike prey on are not evenly distributed. Certain specific areas may be well populated at times, but generally the prey fish are thin on the ground. The shoals, often enormous, move around the loch, their location dependent on the time of year and the availability of their food supply. To sustain themselves the pike have to follow the shoals often moving long distances, so a pike that has to hunt over large areas is a pike in training, muscle-toned and fit. In any part of the world where pike are indigenous, those living in vast clear waters have the same characteristics as Lomond pike; they are large finned, long, lean and fight like demons.

The strong southerly wind continued to funnel down the length of the loch, until the time arrived to pack away our tackle and set off on the long drive home. We had caught some moderate-sized fish, but the legendary monsters had eluded us, as they would so many fine anglers in future years. However our visit hadn't been wasted: we had acquired some valuable first-hand knowledge, had learned about the great difficulty in locating large fish in huge waters and how the vagaries of the highland weather could seriously disrupt the best laid plans, and perhaps most important of all had discovered how our normal English-style pike tackle was no match for the Lomond pike.

For the next few years I became obsessed with Loch Lomond, and made my first return journey to Ardlui the following October. Now the sky was overcast again but the highland air was mild and the wind was less strong than before. The trees by the shoreline and on the lower mountain slopes were clothed in all the tones of yellow, bronze and rich warm browns imaginable, while scarlet berries adorned the rowans; autumn comes early in the Highlands. With winter in the offing, we hoped that the pike would be feeding hard in order to acquire a store of body fat to see them through the cold lean months ahead.

We were now far better equipped, not only with more suitable tackle but with a variety of baits including lively deep-bodied roach lovingly transported in aerated containers, some blue-backed, red-eyed herrings and some fresh plump mackerel whose silvery flanks gleamed irridescent. Returning to the inlet we noticed that the bottom weed had died back due to the fall in water temperature. Now it was possible to cast our herrings and mackerel so that they would sink slowly and lie on the bottom, an easy meal for any pike encountering them.

For the first days we fished our baits thus, and while waiting we often let our gaze wander from the red-topped floats to linger on the wild beauty of the landscape. The tangled branches of a great tree that had fallen in the loch sprouted from the surface; stripped of bark the bleached limbs hung over the grey water. Stark bare outcrops of menacing rock pierced the surface, while the heather and bracken-clad mountain slopes seemed to press down upon us. It was a remote, wild and lonely place. We caught pike on our first day though even the small ones fought with a power and ferocity that was hardly credible. I tussled with one fish that should have been immense, going by the strength of its leaping, twisting fight, but although it was immaculate—a gem of a fish, dazzlingly marked and streamlined to perfection—it was a typically lean loch pike and weighed 18 lb exactly.

On the second evening the sky cleared and the air temperature plummeted. In the morning we awoke to find that the grass crackled underfoot, so sharp had been the overnight frost. As usual we sallied forth full of enthusiasm, but throughout the day our baits were ignored. Undoubtedly the sudden drop in temperature had affected the pike and they were disinclined to feed. We should have expected as much, for pike behave exactly the same in England—but in England we knew that once the fish became accustomed to the change in conditions they would feed again, at first spasmodically, then for short periods often coinciding with the slight rise in temperature, at mid-day. We hoped that the loch pike would show the same behaviour trait, but to our disappointment we had to end our stay before we could find out.

Around this time the South Yorks Specimen Group ceased to exist and for nearly two years I fished alone. Then I had an invitation to join the Hallamshire Specimen. In 1976 I teamed up with the Group's secretary Mick Mulhearne and another member Ian Saxby. Both these anglers were as keen as I to get to grips with a monster loch pike, for we were convinced that such fish were there for the catching! Success was sure to come, it was just a matter of time. During my earlier correspondence with Richard Walker he had written of an enormous pike that his fishing companion Fred Buller had hooked and lost while fishing in the same area that Tommy Morgan had taken his 47-lb fish. While Fred was playing his pike it swam past the boat. Richard saw every inch of that great fish clearly, and watched in amazement as it tore away shaking its vast head. Richard was the greatest, most knowledgeable angler of his generation, and in his carefully considered opinion, Fred's fish had he boated it, would have weighed at least a stupendous 50 lb. We shall never know, for the knot joining the line to the wire trace gave way under the immense pressure, so that truly enormous pike—surely with a disdainful swirl—swam free, never to be seen again.

Mick and I had already fished by Balmaha and in particular the famed Endrick bank, the scene of Tommy Morgan's triumph and where Fred Buller had so nearly made angling history, and were keen to go back there. We were so keen that we just could not wait through the dreary winter months and decided on a pioneering winter trip. We had heard that in the harsh extremes of Canadian winters, pike were caught by fishing through holes bored in the thick ice covering the Great Lakes. Pike are caught in a similar fashion in the northern states of the USA, Russia and Scandinavia. If pike fed in such low temperatures there, we reasoned that the Lomond pike would do likewise, and besides much of Lomond's open water is never icebound.

As the time to head north arrived a heavy fall of snow blanketed Yorkshire. We became dismayed, certain that we had taken a winter break from work to no avail. With trepidation I phoned the AA for a report on road conditions, but was reassured to hear that the M62, the M6 and the route to Glasgow were clear, although the few miles further north to Lomond might be difficult if more snow was to fall. Mick and I decided to risk it and at 6 pm on a bitterly cold evening we piled a mountain of gear into Mick's car. During loading some water slopped out of the livebait container onto the road. It was so cold that it froze immediately. This called for yet another assessment of the appalling conditions. If it was that cold in Yorkshire we wondered how much colder it was going to be in the highlands. A keen angler's mentality must be bewildering to those who have never held a fishing rod. Anyone with a modicum of common sense would have abandoned the trip and retired to the warmth of his home. But we, with only a qualm or two, which we had no intention of communicating to each other, decided to press on regardless of the weather. Amazingly the drive north was uneventful, and some six hours later we arrived at the home of our old friends Mr and Mrs Fraser who plied us with hot drinks before showing us to our caravan where we were relieved to see there was already a welcoming fire lit.

After setting the alarm clock to wake us half an hour before dawn, we turned in. During the night it had snowed with a vengeance and we awoke to find the ground inches deep in a crisp white mantle. As it grew light the mirror-like loch surface was smoking with frost that hung heavily, like the pall of coalfire smoke that blankets a northern town on a cold winter morning. Clutching a bottle of whisky for Jim Pairman, boatyard proprietor at Balmaha and another friend of long standing, we lugged the tackle and baits to the landing stage. Jim and I reminisced for a while, discussed our prospects then set about freeing two ice-bound boats. We needed two, for Ian had also joined us.

The main body of the loch was ice free and soon we were heading out of the boatyard bound for the Endrick bank. A north-easterly breeze had quickly cleared the frost fog, and as the wind increased in strength it became agonisingly cold. Mick and Ian shared one boat while I alone in the other, watched the depths recorded on the echo sounder, and searched for and found the bank. As the anchor gripped and the boat swung round, waves slapping against the rake of the stem, I started to fish. I cast a small chub deadbait upwind so that it rested on the bottom where the base of the bank levelled off. Satisfied that the bait was exactly where I wanted it to lie

I released the spool of the reel so that a pike could run off with the bait, then engaged the ratchet so that I should have audible warning. The second rod I baited with a lively roach, suspended under a float. 'One deadbait and one plump roach, gives them a choice' I muttered to myself as I lowered the roach over the side to check that the bait was suspended at

the depth I wanted. I watched the float cock, riding the waves as the roach swam down and away. Then so unexpectedly that I was amazed, the float disappeared as well. I found myself playing a pike, and though it was only a small fish, and in spite of the intense cold it fought hard. For a pike of only $9^1/_2$ lb it put up a most spirited performance. It really did not matter what size that pike was, what was important was that I had proved my theory that Lomond pike could be caught in the depths of winter. I was elated, the biting cold forgotten, for here was the living proof lying in the bottom of the boat.

The pike was unhooked and returned, and I watched it glide down until its long sinuous shape faded. Next the ratchet on my other reel began to click. The chub deadbait had been taken. Grabbing the rod I set the hooks, and immediately the rod was fully bent and I had to yield yard after yard of line. Normally pike caught in winter do not fight hard, so my experience of English fish had taught me. But this pike was not obeying the rules. It fought with great power, running fast and stripping yards of line from the reel. All sense of time is lost when endeavouring to control large fish, but after what seemed an age I glimpsed the long, lean shape of a much larger fish than I had previously caught in the loch. For a second I saw the great spread of tail then yet again it drove deep down. The runs became shorter, fatigue began to tell and eventually I guided this magnificent specimen of a loch pike into the folds of the large landing net. Perhaps shaking a little, and certainly nearly as exhausted as the pike, I carefully unhooked the big 20-lb Lomond fish. Scaling $22^1/_2$ lb it was one of the most spectacular pike I had ever clapped eyes on. In both colour and shape it was superlative; magnificence lay at my feet. As quickly as possible I gently lowered the fish into the icy water. Who would have thought that my largest Lomond pike to date would be caught when conditions appeared to be so unfavourable?

The following day Mick joined me in the boat and we had several pike to just under 17 lb. The cold north-east wind never ceased but neither did we, we had come to catch pike and only the most appalling weather would prevent us from pursuing our quest. In these cold conditions, we found that the pike fed from first light until 11 am. Then all activity ceased and it seemed that fishing for them during the rest of the day was a waste of time. The habits of fish can be unpredictable; just when you think you have discovered a pattern of behaviour something occurs to upset that pattern.

On the morning of our last day even though the weather was similar to the other days, our baits remained untouched. I became despondent, and was quite convinced that we would return at dusk without a fish to either

Derrick Amies with a 21^1/$_2$-lb Lomond pike taken on livebait.

boat. Then, mid-afternoon, a little pike chased one of my livebaits up to the surface. Seeing how small the pike was I quickly reeled in and drew the bait away leaving the bemused pike wondering where it had gone. Gradually my bait worked back into the same area and the float disappeared. Thinking that the little pike was the culprit, I struck quickly; the rod was wrenched into a hoop and I found myself connected yet again to a sizeable fish that fought as only Lomond pike can, testing both the angler and his tackle to the limits. She was a beautifully proportioned 23¾-lb fish in the peak of condition.

Placing her carefully in the retaining sack we quickly rowed to the nearby shore in order to take some photographs. Once on the bank I started to unsack the pike but some of the mesh had become entangled in her teeth. My hands were numb with the cold and as I fumbled, the pike re-opened her huge jaws and clamped down hard on my thumb and index finger. A pike's grip is like a vice and the pain was excruciating. Of course I could have killed the pike, but as I always return my fish, this had to be the last resort, only to be used if I could not extricate my hand in any other way.

Mick thought and acted quickly; whipping off his hat, he rolled it up and jammed it into the pike's mouth forcing it open. I then saw that one of her razor sharp teeth has passed right through the underside of my finger to penetrate the nail. Freeing my finger was a painful process but once the pike had been returned to the water, I had to suffer many wisecracks and horrific predictions as to the state my hand would be in in the morning. Back at base, I anaesthetized myself with more whisky than was good for me, partly in celebration and partly to kill the pain. My friends were quite correct in their assumption that I would be suffering the following morning, but they were incorrect in one respect—it was my head that was painful now, not my finger!

During the following years we continued to fish the loch, exploring new areas and gradually adding to our hard-won knowledge. We fished in the bays off Luss on the western shore and discovered areas where the pike collected in the spring for their annual spawning ritual. We also found that the loch pike generally fed in the early mornings or evenings and not too well at other times unless the light value was low due to overcast skies. During these visits, even if the fishing was slow at times, we always had the magnificent scenery to admire, and we became attuned to the ever-changing moods of Lomond and her surrounding mountains. Sometimes they were snowclad, at others they were covered in green bracken and purple heather, and occasionally we glimpsed the herds of red deer grazing the slopes. Binoculars were as much part of our tackle as rods. Wildfowl swept over us and once we watched a majestic golden eagle quarter the mountain slopes, hunting mountain hares.

But even though more and more anglers fished for the pike of Lomond, no one ever encountered one of the great fishes of legend. Some told of great fish hooked and lost but then as loch pike fight with such power, those fish although large were probably not as large as people thought—the pull on the rod tip is out of all proportion to their weight. Such stories only added further to the myth though and encouraged yet more anglers to trek north.

In the late 1970s Kevin Clifford, writing in the angling press, spread a seed of doubt concerning Loch Lomond and its reputation for huge pike. He pointed out that after some of the nation's most experienced pike anglers had fished Lomond for years, the best fish to be caught was the $34^1/2$-lb pike of Slim Baxter. My best fish weighed $28^1/4$ lb. Kevin thought that English waters, that were now beginning to produce really big pike, would be a better proposition for a record pike than Lomond. So far he has been proved correct for a fish over 40 lb in weight has been caught in the Norfolk Broads and another has just recently been taken from an Essex reservoir.

Are there enormous pike in Loch Lomond? No one can say for sure. Until one is caught the argument will continue. Some are still convinced such fish exist, others discount the possibility. Vic Bellars, who has helped me with this book, has a theory as to why, if monstrous pike still swim in the loch, no one has caught one. Although Vic has never fished Loch Lomond and therefore does not expect anyone to take his ideas too seriously, he has been fishing for pike for over 50 years and has rather more knowledge of pike behaviour in huge deep waters than modern-day young anglers have yet to acquire. Vic suggests that those who have fished in Lomond have fished in the wrong place and at the wrong depth. He freely admits that is a bold statement from one who has seen Lomond only from a train! In America and in Holland pike can suspend up to 60 feet down in really deep water, and can lie comfortably on the bottom in water of similar depth or deeper. Pike as a species and particularly the huge ones can become stressed when water temperatures rise above 60 °F. To escape to cooler water, a pike will go deep where the temperature is lower.

In winter the shallow water will be coldest, so at that time of the year it would not be too uncomfortable and one would expect that large pike

The northern end of Loch Lomond at Ardlui. My first serious pike
session took place here in the mid-sixties.

A 23-lb carp from a Norfolk day-ticket lake.

would not have to lie so deep. Any part of the loch should suit them. Yet even in winter no one seems to have caught a Lomond monster. Vic has a theory on this too. He thinks the really great pike feed almost exclusively on powan. This herring-like fish spends almost all its life in deep water only venturing into the shallows to spawn. (The powan shoals are vast—I once saw a shoal half a mile long swimming along the Endrick bank at spawning time.) So if for most of the year the powan lie deep, 60 or 100 feet down, it then becomes probable that the huge pike lie at the same depth where they would have easy access to a plentiful supply of food. They might move as the shoal moves, but would always stay within reach.

Vic also thinks he knows why the huge pike do not migrate to the spawning areas, for if they did, with all the anglers concentrating there in the spring the law of averages would dictate that at least one would pick up a bait. His theory begins with the fact that large pike are always females; a pike of 50, 60 or even 70 lb would be in the last phase of her life—an old fish. The reproductory urge would have lessened, perhaps at some stage a menopause would have occurred and the ovaries have ceased to function. Such a fish would lose the desire to reproduce so she would not migrate to the spawning beds each spring. This, Vic thinks is the reason why such huge fish do not appear in the shallows, they remain deep down in the loch while the younger fish are left to perpetuate the species.

Most of the pike anglers who have fished in Lomond concentrate on water no deeper than 25 feet. With the modern graph recorders, not only can the powan shoals be located, but any larger fish nearby would show on the display. Every bottom feature can be interpreted, even hundreds of feet down, so with the aid of technology perhaps one day we shall know for certain whether the great pike of Lomond do haunt the dimly-lit depths.

Fish lying so deep could be fished for in two ways: powan or similar-sized fish could be suspended under a float at the same depth or a little below a powan shoal, or, using the sophisticated down-rigger trolling equipment by which Americans catch salmon deep down in the Great Lakes, the deep waters of the loch could be trolled using large artificial lures or deadbaits. Vic thinks the latter method might be productive but until someone tries it we shall never know.

Perhaps *Esox giganticus,* a monster of a fish does really exist, bigger than Tommy Morgan's, bigger even than the Endrick pike. One day we may know for certain, until then Lomond holds its secrets.

Carp: The Queen of The Water

Isaac Walton in that delightful book *The Compleat Angler* first published in 1653 says of the carp that she is 'a stately, a good and very subtil fish'. Walton was not averse to plagiarism, for as was the custom of the day, he borrowed freely from other writers. However, he was forced to rely on his own observations when describing carp and how they could be caught. The words stately and subtle were well chosen for the aldermanic carp is more crafty and cunning than any other fish an angler strives to catch.

Walton, whose longevity was exceptional for the age in which he lived, travelled to counties as far apart as Hampshire and Derbyshire in order to fish. Even in his eighties he thought little of making the tedious journey on horseback from Winchester, in order to beguile the trout and grayling of the Dove with delicate flies of his own tying, cleverly joined to casts made from the hair of horses' tails.

Walton was a strong Royalist but he managed to fish and write of fishing without becoming embroiled in the bitter struggle between King and Parliament. His style of writing is perhaps too tedious and inclined to circumlocutory passages for the modern-day angler to stomach, but hidden among the anecdotes, songs and poems, and the advice on dressing fish for the table, descriptions of archaic tackle and the virtues of milkmaids, are little gems of advice on how to catch a fish. While this advice has tended to be ignored, much is sound and born of Walton's own experiences, even though when he wrote this, the carp had not long been established in England, and very few waters had been stocked.

Any angler today, following his suggestions would not suffer any undue handicap and would certainly succeed. Apart from natural baits such as worms and gentles, the latter surely a much more pleasant term for maggots, Walton advocated the use of paste baits rolled into pellets. As for the ingredients, he said these could be legion, but the best were either meat based or sweetened with sugar or honey. Both will still tempt carp, and if those ancient carp had a sweet tooth, so do their counterparts today, for many of our modern carp baits contain a sweetening agent. He was certain that maggots could be made even more attractive if allowed to wriggle

Carp fishing in mid-summer.

through sweetened bran. Only recently have anglers begun to realize that flavouring maggots can make them more attractive to fish than when in their natural state, yet the old master was doing just that in the seventeenth century.

Walton said that a carp angler, and he used the term as if those who fished for carp were a race apart from ordinary anglers, must fish early or late; also, that bait should be thrown into the water several times before the angler attempts to fish. If Walton realised the value of pre-baiting, his most intriguing suggestion was to pre-bait with grains. So that remarkable man used particle baits, unheard of until the Sixties, when particles in the form of sweetcorn became one of the most popular baits. And there have been some who have baited up a swim and fished with stewed wheat, no doubt thinking that they had thought of the idea. Old Walton knew a thing or two about the art of angling. Only the limitations imposed by his inadequate tackle and the shortage of carp prevented him from catching more carp than he did. His final piece of advice to the carp angler was to cultivate the virtue of patience, for as he said, 'the carp is a crafty fish'. If much has changed since Walton's day, the habits of carp have not; they are crafty fish indeed.

Fish are singularly lacking in brains and carp are no exception, but all fish compensate for this deficiency by having superbly acute instincts. By far the most developed of these is the instinct to survive. From the moment fish hatch from the egg as tiny alevins and become fry as the yolk sac is absorbed, they live in an environment where eating or being eaten affects every second of their precarious lives. So from the moment of birth a fish is endowed with an inherent instinctive cunning, and as Walton said, the carp is the most crafty and cunning of them all.

Carp are quick to learn from experience, and furthermore seem able to remember for rather longer than other species. For instance, a carp which discovers a food source that tastes good can lead to an unpleasant experience—being caught—will become progressively more difficult to catch on that bait. Carp also associate the area where they were hooked with danger and although they may frequent such an area again they will only feed there with circumspection, if at all. It can take months, often a year or even longer before the memory fades and a carp will feed once more on a substance that it once associated with danger. This also affects other carp in the same lake. Once a number of carp in a lake have been caught on a particular bait it is not long before all the carp, including those that have not been caught, to avoid eating that bait. In fact they show every sign of alarm when they come across or even scent such baits; they know instinctively that they are dangerous. We know of course that a carp which has been caught and returned to the water doesn't swim around telling its companions that those nice-tasting little balls are really bad news! Yet it has communicated with its fellows to the extent that all the carp in that fishery avoid such baits like the plague.

Fish like mammals involuntarily emit a scent when frightened. We likewise sweat when terrified; the phrase 'He broke out in a cold sweat' beloved by many a thriller writer aptly describes this natural process. The sensory faculties of carp are far more highly developed than our own, and can detect the fear scent emanating from one of their own species over long distances. We are aware that a carp when it sees or smells a bait which it has been caught on will become agitated and frightened. The fear scent is emitted which is sensed by other carp nearby, so those carp become agitated too; agitated fish are disinclined to feed and will avoid the area where they detect the fear scent. In this way carp in a particular water learn to avoid the carp anglers' baits.

When carp cease to take baits of a certain colour or flavour, these baits, in the parlance of carp anglers, are known as 'blown' so anglers are forever experimenting with new baits and new ways of presenting them, so as not to arouse the carp's suspicions. The angler's superior intelligence, however, seems to be equally matched by the carp's instinctive cunning allied to its highly developed sensory perception.

That is why carp fishing is such a challenge, carp are not easy to catch and there are many anglers so obsessed with trying to outwit this wily fish, that they fish for nothing else. So Walton's 'subtil' carp, in spite of the technological advances are more than holding their own against the wiles of the modern carp angler.

This stately fish is not of a species indigenous to this country. When the first carp was slipped into an English pond is unknown, but at least we can guess why it was introduced. In medieval times transport from the coast to the interior was by pack horse, so it was quite impractical for sea fish to arrive at their destination fit for human consumption. Those living far from the sea, if they needed fresh fish, had to rely on those they could catch from rivers and lakes. Carp, as now, were a popular food on the Continent, better tasting than other coarse fish, so perhaps an enterprising citizen having tasted a fat carp cooked in wine and herbs while abroad, decided to ship a few back to England in order to stock his own waters. If so, the experiment was successful; it was soon realised that carp could survive, grow and even spawn when the temperature soared in the warm summer months. So landowners, and in particular the ecclesiastical establishments, the monasteries, excavated stew ponds and stocked them with carp, tench and sometimes bream. All we actually know concerning the introduction of carp into England is that they were brought in prior to 1496. For in 'The treatyse of Fysshynge with an Angle' in that year by Wynkynde de Worde in the second edition of the *Boke of St Albans,* Dame Juliana Berners says of the carp 'but there have been but few in England'. That at least proves that there were some carp to fish for when that piscatorial lady went fishing with an angle.

Walton, in the seventeenth century was of the opinion that carp had been in the country for at least one hundred years, and quotes a verse from Sir Richard Baker's chronicle to prove his theory:

'Hops and turkies, carps and beer
came into England all in a year.'

Turkeys were unknown until Europeans started to colonize North America and must have followed carp. As for beer, I think the medieval yeoman had been long acquainted with strong ale long before the first carp swam in an English lake.

The carp of medieval England, and those that Walton knew, were very different from the huge hog-backed and often pot-bellied fish that indolently bask a summer's day away in so many of our waters now. The wild carp of old was a slim, fully-scaled, bronze-hued fish, very chub-like in appearance and slower growing than modern-day fish. A wild carp of 10 lb, if it ever reached such a size before it was popped in the pan would have been considered huge, and a 20-lb fish would have been a source of wonder to the anglers of old.

There are still one or two small isolated ponds and lakes that contain a pure strain of the old wild, chub-like carp now called 'wildies' to distinguish them from the mirror, leather or fully-scaled common carp. These latter are the huge fish that today's battalions of carp anglers seek, striving to catch 'twenties' and 'thirties' and even making long journeys abroad in an endeavour to catch even more gargantuan fish. Many of these anglers pay scant attention to the wildies, but these smaller fish are just as difficult to catch as their far larger cousins. A wild carp, be it only three or four pounds in weight will, when hooked, fight furiously, tearing through the water like a wayward torpedo. There has been many an angler quietly fishing for roach or bream, unaware of the presence of these small wild carp, who has hooked a fish that within seconds has left him bemused and shattered, with the broken line fluttering from his rod top. The common carp being larger in girth and deeper in body but otherwise in all respects similar to the wildie is the carp most prized by today's carp anglers.

It was pressure put on angling club committees by their members that led to the stocking of many waters with the fast-growing strains of carp reared by pisciculturalists on the Continent. A few were introduced here before the last war but the main stocking occurred in the immediate post-war years. As more and more of these continental fish were placed in the canals, ponds, lakes and gravel pits, they led to the near demise of the wildies, for the new arrivals bred readily with the ancient stock, making it difficult now to tell if a fish which exhibits all the traits of a wildie is a pure-bred fish at all.

It was only during the first quarter of this century that anglers actually went fishing for carp intentionally. Before then carp were considered quite uncatchable on rod and line, not least because the fishing tackle then in vogue was totally inadequate for dealing with such heavy hard-fighting fish. But to the amazement of the angling world at the time, the first 20-lb carp was caught in the Thames at Wallingford, and later John Bickerdyke, famous Victorian angler, mentions in his writings a 23-lb fish caught from Broadwater Pond in Surrey.

From 1911 to 1928 a group of carp fishing pioneers calling themselves the Red Spinners set about trying to catch a carp then known to swim in Cheshunt reservoir. Their records for those 19 years show that they caught 22 carp weighing more than 10 lb. That shows what dedicated carp anglers those stalwarts were, they must have fished day after day without a bite. One of the Red Spinners' bait innovations was to fish with small cooked potatoes. Potatoes have been the downfall of many a carp since, but although most British carp anglers now give such a bait scant consideration the humble 'boilie' is still successfully used in Holland. The culmination of the Red Spinner exploits was the capture by John Andrews of a 20 lb 3-oz fish that was recognised as the official record. These successes were few and far between however because no-one was prepared to experiment with baits, other than bread paste, potato or worms and the pre-war carp anglers were unaware of a carp's learning capacity.

One July day in 1920 Albert Buckley was fishing for roach in Mapperley Reservoir near Ilkeston. Mapperley was noted for its shoals of large roach so Albert was using suitably fine tackle, for few roach are caught that exceed 3 lb and such are exceptional fish. His tackle consisted of a $2^1/4$-lb breaking strain line and a number 10 hook. Old Isaac Walton would have approved of his bait—brown bread sweetened with honey. Albert caught his roach; two one-pounders and one huge one of over three. It matters not that those fish were certainly hybrids, but these fine fish were as nothing compared with what was to follow. Albert also caught six carp, I doubt if anyone has caught so many in one day, but one of those carp was huge for those times, weighing in at 26 lb. The angling world was ablaze, it was an astounding achievement, and the carp record that had stood for 14 years was shattered.

Albert Buckley's exploits showed other anglers keen to catch carp, that at last the uncatchable had become catchable. It was however to be many years before the uncatchable myth was finally laid to rest. Magnificent as was Albert's carp catch, few in succeeding years could emulate his success, and in fact it proved to be a retrograde step in the development of carp fishing techniques. Because Albert used fine line of a low breaking strain, since he was after roach, other anglers imagined that the only way to catch carp was to fish likewise. Obviously Albert was more skilled in playing large fish on light tackle than many others, but endeavouring to catch carp thus was courting disaster. Large carp were hooked, but charged off into lily beds, thick weed or buried themselves in a tangle of underwater tree roots and so people were still convinced that catching carp was nearly impossible. Who can blame them? There just wasn't any suitable tackle available, and certainly strong forged hooks were unobtainable.

The Fisherman's Bedside Book by Denys Watkins-Pitchford published under the *nom de plume* 'BB' in 1946 led to an upsurge of interest in carp angling and the desire of angling club members to have their waters stocked with carp.

However, carp fishing was still in its infancy when one man alone not only changed the face of angling but revolutionised the embryo carp scene as well. He not only announced that carp could be caught, he then set about proving the truth of his statement by catching them. That man was Richard Walker already briefly mentioned in the chapter on pike. Richard was cultured and articulate and a fine engineer. Because there was no tackle in existence capable of dealing with so powerful a fish as carp, he designed and made the specialist equipment necessary to catch them. For twenty-five years Richard wrote a weekly feature for *Angling Times,* and his theories, now widely promulgated, had a profound influence on his readers and also the fishing tackle manufacturers. To give but one instance, he complained year after year about the inadequacies of hook design, until eventually sharp, small-barbed and immensely strong forged hooks were reluctantly manufactured. Richard designed, then constructed beautifully balanced hexagonal rods from split cane. This required great skill and patience, but the result, the original Mk IV Carp Rod was a precision tool that could in the right hands cope with any carp, however large. He also made his own large landing net and for night fishing used his inventive engineering capabilities to produce the first electronic bite alarm, the 'buzzer'. As a just reward Richard caught from Redmire Pool a magnificent common carp of 44 lb. This record stood for years, until comparatively recently Chris Yates landed a 50-lb fish from the same water.

At last the uncatchable carp were being caught with regularity. Richard and like-minded anglers including 'BB' formed the Carp Catchers Club. Membership was by invitation and sensibly there were no rules and no subscription. Richard became Secretary and encouraged the members to share their knowledge and experience which was freely available by letter and leaflet. The word spread far and wide. All this happened in the early fifties and in the next two decades anglers were catching carp from many waters and the face of angling had changed irrevocably. Until then Coarse anglers, so named to differentiate them from the Game anglers, those who specialised in trout and salmon, fished in the main for any species that took their fancy. Now the ranks of the Coarse anglers were splitting and an entirely new type of specialist angler appeared on the scene: the dedicated, dyed in the wool carp man.

Other organisations were formed: the British Carp Study Group,

shortly to be followed by the Carp Society. New fisheries proliferated and more and more carp waters were managed on a syndicate basis. The demand for carp waters became insatiable. Lakes were purchased, stocked with carp and turned into syndicates, at a price. Coarse fishing, the traditional recreation of the working man had suddenly become big business. Once trout and salmon beats, the prerogative of the wealthy were way beyond the means of the Coarse angler, now the price of carp fishing was becoming almost as expensive. Coarse angling had changed beyond recognition in a few short years and this was entirely due to the increasing popularity of one fish, the carp.

Such cataclysmic changes in the attitude of a minority of Coarse fishermen has been to the advantage of many but to the detriment of others. Better and better carp fishing, together with far more waters available to the carp angler is an obvious benefit. But while the working man is now more affluent, and has his own car to travel to a good fishery many miles from his home, others, particularly the young and the old, have such fishing denied them; they can no longer afford it. Certainly some bad feeling has been aroused; when anglers used to fishing their local waters suddenly find these waters have become expensive syndicates, the annual fee far beyond what they can afford, they are quite reasonably angry. There is a danger that the present policies of syndication could lead to deep divisions among anglers in the future.

Carp fisheries are valuable, and quite legally can be purchased by anyone prepared to pay the large sums such waters can command. No-one can blame a fishery owner for managing his water so as to recoup his investment and eventually make a profit. Many carp waters are extremely well managed; they have been planted and landscaped, becoming not only fine fisheries but havens for wildlife. This is certainly to the credit of the carp anglers and for good or evil, the influence of the carp men is changing the sport of angling out of all recognition.

It used to take many years for an angler to acquire the skills necessary to catch large fish from a variety of waters, from tranquil lakes to swift flowing rivers. But now a young person, if he has the means, can equip himself with the latest tackle, accessories and baits. If he fishes a water containing big fish, by piling in the baits and fishing over them he will in all probability land the fish of his dreams. There are many of these instant anglers; some become successful and versatile but others remain one-method anglers. I make no criticism of such people, we are all free to fish as we please, but I feel they deny themselves a greater understanding of the fascinating subtleties inherent in the wider aspects of angling. For there is always another goal, another challenge to overcome and after a lifetime's fishing there is still so much to learn.

As for the carp itself, together with pike and the few European catfish, the wels, it is the largest and most powerful coarse fish an angler is likely to tangle with. Many fisheries contain fish of over 20 lb, 30-lb fish are not all that rare and of course, much larger carp are known to exist. On the Continent and in the USA where carp have been introduced, they can reach immense weights. In Lake Cassien in southern France English anglers have caught many large carp; already the 70-lb barrier has been exceeded. The effect such exploits have had on European anglers has benefited the British tackle trade as demand for specialist tackle grows apace. The carp anglers are changing and influencing the attitudes of foreign anglers as they have in this country. It is now recognised by anglers abroad and even in North America that British anglers specialising in the pursuit of large fish have evolved tackle and techniques far in advance of their own.

When I caught my first carp many of the modern innovative techniques used by today's anglers had not been invented. I fished for carp much as I did for tench, only the bait was different. Carp would however take surface baits, the presentation of floating baits to fish that could be seen was one of the most exciting ways of fishing that I had ever encountered.

My first foray after carp was at Ravensfield Ponds in South Yorkshire. This fishery consisted of a group of three waters, two of four acres or so, the smallest only an acre in extent. All three had been stocked with mirror carp; they had not been in the lakes long enough to become heavyweights but a few were 'doubles' that is fish weighing in excess of 10 lb. Ravensfield was an exclusive fishery but I was fortunate in that I could fish there as a guest of one of the members. The lakes were very picturesque nestling in a small valley close to Rotherham, an oasis amid an industrial landscape. Much of the surface of these waters was covered in dense beds of arrowhead and potamogeton, the narrow-leaved water lily. The margins were boggy and overgrown with reeds and flag iris, it was a haven of tranquillity. The myth of the carp's uncatchability was a belief still held by some of the anglers who fished at Ravensfield who thought that trying to catch them was a waste of time. Certainly they were difficult to catch but carp always are and this only made me more determined to prove these doubters wrong. The very few who had caught a Ravensfield carp had succeeded by using breadcrust floating on the surface. Crust is buoyant, remains floating for long periods and carp like it, but unfortunately so do coots, moorhens, ducks and swans. These can become such a nuisance as to make fishing with crust impossible. These hungry fowl can, however, be fooled. The crust is anchored by a pear-shaped weight which has a swivelled eye set into its narrow end. This universally popular weight designed by Richard Walker is called an Arlesley Bomb. The line is passed through the eye; once the bomb is lying on the lake bottom, the crust, being buoyant, will draw line through the eye as it floats upward to the surface. When some inquisitive water fowl approaches the crust the angler reels in a little line so the crust sinks. Usually the bird is nonplussed, and swims off disconsolately, then, by releasing line, the angler makes the crust pop up to the surface. Eventually some enterprising fowl, nearly always a coot, ceases to be put off and dives after the disappearing crust—there's no answer to that!

When using freelined crust with only a hook tied to the line, I greased the line, so like the crust it floated too. A greased line lying in the surface film is far more visible that when it is underwater, so I left a little length of line near the crust untreated so that it would sink. Carp will happily slurp down crusts but never those with the line floating right by them, for it is far too detectable.

One evening I had thrown a few loose crusts into the swim followed by another attached to the hook. The loose offerings were designed to entice some carp from the sheltering potamogeton beds. While there might not have been any sign of fish, once the crusts had been in the water for a few minutes the carp seemed to sense their presence and swam out to investigate. The breeze had caused the crusts to drift up against a reed bed some twenty-five yards away and a number of fish had found them and were enthusiastically mopping them up. Even when a crust has been dipped into water for a second or two to give it some extra weight it cannot be cast far, unless the wind is blowing from behind; about fifteen yards is about the most that can be achieved. Carefully and with pent up excitement I placed a fresh crust on the hook, cast out and by manipulating the line aided by a modicum of luck managed to get the bait to drift towards the reeds. I watched the crust, stark white in contrast to the dark water; one fish perhaps scenting this fresh crust, moved out from the reeds and neatly intercepted it. At one moment the crust was bobbing along, then in a split second it had disappeared replaced by a large swirl as the carp sucked it down then turned no doubt in the hope of finding another. Perhaps rather foolishly I was using a light rod and only 4-lb breaking strain line. The next few minutes were hectic; I had never hooked or played a carp before and I was unprepared for the speed and power that fish displayed. I desperately wanted to land that carp, which because of my inadequate tackle I could barely control at all. Luck must have been running my way; against all the odds the fish did not plunge into the lilies and slowly with the utmost care I gently coaxed it nearer and nearer until it was circling under the top of the rod. A few seconds later, trembling with excitement, I lifted my net, complete with carp, ashore. As carp go it was an unexceptional fish weighing just a shade over 6 lb. To me it was a memorable prize—my first carp.

From that moment on, like the carp, I too was hooked, hooked on carp fishing. I read as much as I could of Richard Walker's books and articles, pored through feature after feature in the weekly and monthly angling press, sought advice from other carp anglers in order to acquire as much information as I could on the catching of carp. Not least I began to think up ideas, not only for suitable tackle but what for other baits I might try in order to outwit these wily fish.

I had certainly caught my fish on crust, but it took very little time for the carp to realize that crusts spelled danger. They still wanted them but instead of taking them, they nosed and banged against them until the bread began to disintegrate. As the smaller pieces fell away they ate those but never the piece of crust with the hook in it. For a while the carp could still be caught by passing the line through a crust a couple of times then baiting the hook with a much smaller piece of flake, the fluffy white crumb from the centre of the loaf. As the crust floated, this little piece of flake hung down a few inches below it. When the carp started breaking up the crust and little pieces started sinking, they mistook the flake for one of these. It worked for a time, but eventually carp would have nothing to do with crust at all.

Today carp will take floating baits, but at that time baits such as Pedigree Chum Mixer, Munchies (a cat food) and specially-flavoured commercially produced baits were undreamed of. If the carp wouldn't take crust I had no alternative but to fish for them with baits lying on the bottom. I had previously caught tench with bottom-fished flake, but I reasoned that if the carp were wary of bread on the surface they might feel the same about such a bait wherever they found it. I decided that cheese paste which is made by kneading dampened stale bread and grated cheese together to make a smooth paste would be worth a try, as well as a paste made from uncooked beef sausage meat, stiffened with breadcrumbs and

34

soya flour. Both these baits could be rolled into bait-sized balls, and anglers had begun to catch carp on both concoctions as well as on cubes of tinned luncheon meat which became a popular and successful bait.

I suppose it took me some ten years before I could go carp fishing with any real degree of confidence but not a little time was spent fishing for other species such as barbel and pike.

While I was a member of a specimen group I was able to become a member of a syndicate controlled by Kevin Clifford who was rapidly gaining a nationwide reputation as a fine angler. This water, Cave Castle near Hull had been fished by some of the Hallamshire Specimen Group and they informed me how very difficult it was to tempt any of the carp it contained. Cave Castle was another small water with extensive shallows at one end, and an island. It was, like so many carp lakes, a quiet and peaceful place. It seemed that the carp were not often caught because the water was crystal clear and chock-a-block with natural food. I like a challenge, so I was not unduly perturbed and decided to fish for Cave Castle carp come what may. I also thought that with such a problem two heads might be better than one. I teamed up with Bob Goodison, a kindred spirit and another aspiring carp angler; it was not long before we became firm friends.

We spent a great deal of time planning the downfall of Cave Castle carp, not least trying to think of baits that might wean them away from their more natural diet. By now particle baits were much in vogue in carp-fishing circles. Particles often do well on hard waters. The principle behind their use is to scatter thousands of small baits over much of the lake bottom so the carp cannot fail to find them wherever they swim. Once the carp come to realise that these baits are good to eat, the pre-baiting can be then concentrated, drawing the fish into those swims the angler intends to fish.

One of the most successful particle baits was sweetcorn, but today many exotic varieties of seeds and beans are used. Well-known baits in the early days were haricot beans, chick peas, maple peas and even sultanas. Bob and I decided to use black-eyed beans flavoured with a banana-flavoured cooking essence. The flavour penetrated the beans during cooking; all seed baits must be softened by simmering, for a stomach full of hard uncooked seeds can cause a carp to die. Even when a particle is 'blown' it can be made into a good bait again by changing its flavour and sometimes its colour. Black-eyes can be cooked in canned soup or sweetened with sugar or saccharine, the flavours are unending.

Well before the fishing season commenced on June 16th we carried out a heavy pre-baiting campaign at Cave Castle. We arrived at the lake on the evening of the 15th and having tackled up, waited impatiently for midnight. On the first second of the new day our baits were cast out, the optonic bite alarms adjusted and indicator bobbin set. We had a great deal of faith in our tactics, so we settled back expecting the warning bleep and flashing pinpoint of red light that signalled a carp had taken the bait. As hour after hour passed without so much as a twitch, let alone a bite, our enthusiasm began to wane. It was further deflated when dawn broke and it became light enough to see the glistening broad backs of many carp as they rolled and swirled on the surface. It seemed as if every carp in the lake was congregated in our swim. When carp roll, it is a behaviour pattern that often coincides with feeding and it was patently obvious that those carp were stuffing themselves full of black-eyed beans. It was fascinating watching this hectic activity but it did little to raise our spirits; our bite alarms remained silent, the bobbins hung immobile, our baits were ignored. It was time for a post-mortem. We advanced many theories: perhaps the presentation of the baits was incorrect, the hook length too long, too short. Could they detect the hook, or perhaps see the line? Certainly the line was stronger that I usually used—an 8-lb breaking strain—but this was an essential as some of the Cave Castle carp were large. Since I could clearly see the line in the clear water, I began to think the carp would be able to see it equally as well, and eventually I was convinced that this was the cause of our failure. I also thought that our static method of fishing in one swim for hours without a bite, when it was pretty certain we would never have one, was rather foolish.

The main problem of line visibility was easily solved, instead of allowing it to extend at an angle from the rod tip to the bomb it must lie on the bottom. At the same time we would bait up a number of swims; if carp activity was seen in any one of them we could instantly move in and fish. I baited up an area of very shallow water varying between just twelve and thirty inches deep. It was an unusual decision but I had seen carp in these shallows during our pre-season baiting sessions. This time I put the bait in the swim in a number of piles so any fish entering the area could not fail to see them. I lengthened the hook length to four feet, cast out then scattered a few beans in the vicinity of my bait. In the clear water I could see the piles of beans and even the loose ones around the bait. I placed the rod in the rests but did not tighten up to the bomb, but allowed the line to sink to the bottom. It hung vertically from the rod tip but that part lying on the bottom I could not discern. In order to tell me if a carp took the bait I watched the line hanging from the rod; if it lifted and straightened it could only mean one thing, a bite. I sat quietly, trying not to move or fidget for the bait was not far from the margin, and in such shallow water any carp nearby would be sure to see or sense my presence.

I had been glancing from time to time at the piles of bait and wondering if I had been wise to fish in such shallow water when the broad, blue-grey shape of a large carp materialised and glided towards a pile of bait. I cannot imagine a more nerve-tingling situation, no words of mine can even attempt to describe the sensation, the anticipation as with my hand hovering over the rod handle I watched that carp as it moved slowly towards my baited hook. That fish, which I estimated would weigh some 15 lb, hoovered up some loose beans, worked its way through one of the small piles, moved on and started to pick up the loose offerings by my bait. The tension increased, a mixture of elation and doubt: one second I was sure the carp would take the bait, the next I felt it would ignore it. The line hanging limp from the rod tip suddenly straightened, I lifted the rod from the rests, it arched into a semi-circle, the water surface heaved, that carp had made a mistake. A carp hooked in shallow water close to the bank bolts for deep water in order to get as far away as possible from where it was hooked. In spite of the relatively strong line I had to allow the fish to charge off to the middle of the lake. I was very anxious to land a Cave Castle carp, difficult fish by reputation, so I handled the fish carefully, resisting the temptation to hustle it towards the landing net. When at last I carried the heavy dripping net ashore, my estimate of 15 lb was inaccurate by 4 oz. That carp, a mirror in excellent condition scaled 14 lb 12 oz.

After all the commotion I did not expect another fish to investigate the shallows for some time, but I cast out a fresh bait and scattered some more beans around it, just in case. After years of carp fishing, which often involved hours of waiting behind my rods I was surprised to see another carp arrive within minutes; it started to clear up as many beans as possible only to suffer the same fate as its predecessor. Slightly smaller, it was still a fine double-figure carp of 13 lb. To outwit two carp within so short a period of time, from such a hard water as Cave Castle I felt was quite an accomplishment, and I must admit I was rather pleased with myself, particularly so because I had succeeded by finding the key to the problem that had defeated so many others. As expected, the carp soon began to view black-eyed beans with suspicion. Because particles had done so well we decided to continue using them; it remained to find a bait that the carp would appreciate. We chose polished maple peas, cooked until soft, then pre-baited as we had done with the black-eyes. To cast maples any distance we had to use some weight on the line. The smallest Arlesley would suffice, but while it was just right for the distances we needed to cast, we very quickly discovered an unexpected hazard. The carp took kindly to the maples but also, because the bombs were much the same size, started picking them up in mistake for the peas. When I substituted a small barrel lead, normally used when spinning artificial lures and very different in shape from the bomb, the trouble ceased.

Bob and I soon came to know every facet of Cave Castle lake, the variations in depth, the changes in the nature of the bottom, the carp's favoured feeding areas and how the fish reacted to climatic change. By the end of the season I had landed 15 doubles plus two superb, fully-scaled common carp of 18 lb. Bob had done equally well and between us we had caught so many carp that nobody thereafter could truthfully say that the Cave Castle carp were hard to catch. The Cave Castle experience had boosted my confidence, and I felt sure that given the time on any water I would eventually be able to catch its carp. Strange as it appears, the confident angler seems to catch the most fish. There's no logical explanation as to why this should be so, but it is a truism that has been proved so often as to seem uncanny.

In the succeeding seasons I fished new waters, travelling as far afield as Cheshire, Nottinghamshire, and Lincolnshire. Rod Hutchinson who was at that time gaining the reputation as one of the country's finest carp anglers (one he still holds) was just forming a bait business. Rod and I fished a small lake in Lincolnshire where it is possible to hire a caravan beside the water. This was another water where the carp were certainly experienced in the ways of anglers. I tried out a new paste bait made from soaked trout pellets stiffened with fish meal as well as Rod's exotically flavoured varieties. Rod, who seemed to have acquired a reputation along with his many other admirable ones of being a serious drinker, was one of the very first to have exploited particle baits to the full.

As night fishing was not allowed we naturally ended up in the local inn most evenings, and enthusiastically sampled the local brew. Even after these heavy nights, I had several common carp to 13 lb, and my best ever, a longed-for 'twenty' of 22 lb 9 oz.

Once I came to live in Norfolk with its wealth of fishing for so many other species, carp were temporarily forsaken, and I concentrated more on tench and the barbel of the Wensum. However, I did carp fish in a notoriously hard water near Norwich, Taverham No 3, a gravel pit which is mentioned more fully in the Tench chapter. I was now helping to promote a range of carp baits marketed by Clive Diedrich, yet another nationally known carp angler. One memorable morning a letter arrived from Clive. He said that he had leased the most famous carp water in the country. Redmire Pool near Ross-on-Wye was where Richard Walker had caught his 44-lb fish and Chris Yates had taken his staggering 50-lb fish. Clive asked if I would be interested in fishing at Redmire a little later in the season. To use that hackneyed contemporary phrase I was 'over the moon'. Redmire was without doubt the carp angler's Mecca. For years rumours had been circulating that it contained one or perhaps two enormous fish. Indeed syndicate members of old had told their friends that they had actually seen gigantic carp. Every carp angler's ambition was to receive an invitation to fish this renowned water. Redmire was so exclusive that carp anglers could only join the syndicate by recommendation and vacancies were few. Besides, the annual subscription was beyond the scope of many. Even those in the syndicate could not fish when they liked for there a strict rota system in force, with so much time allotted to each member. I really was in a daze after reading Clive's letter and from then on I could think of little else besides Redmire Pool.

Another fine angler Tony Miles had been allocated the same few days as myself, so we decided to work as a team rather than individually. At last on a Tuesday morning I set out on the long drive from Norfolk and picked up the M4 heading west for the Severn Bridge. I hardly noticed the hours passing, my mind was full of Redmire, its great carp and all the famous anglers who had fished there. Redmire was a secluded water well off the beaten track so Clive had given me some precise directions on its location. Either he was looking at the map upside down or imagined I would enter the area from another direction. Whatever the reason I took a wrong turning and became hopelessly lost. I found myself in a little village so I called in at the post office and after not a little persuasion, a very reluctant post mistress pointed me in the right direction. At first I was a little nonplussed by my reception but then it dawned on me that the good lady had no doubt suffered the enquiries of all kinds of fishermen trying to discover the whereabouts of Redmire over the years.

Passing a cottage and negotiating a gate, the lane climbed steeply until I reached the top of the rise. A beautiful little valley was spread out before me and nestling among the trees I could see a small lake, Redmire Pool. The view was so entrancing, the Herefordshire countryside so verdant, that I sat enthralled. Perhaps fifteen minutes passed before my reverie was interrupted by the sound of a voice floating up from the valley. It was Tony who had noticed my car so I drove down to the compound to greet him. Ushering me through a small gate and urging me not to slam the car door, for he had been watching some carp in that part of the lake adjacent to the car parking area, we stood gazing at the most famous of all carp waters; for me it was a magical moment.

We then spent at least two hours creeping round the pool's perimeter, even climbing trees in an endeavour to see some of the large carp. I saw some at the shallow end. They were big. All my expectations were being realized. I wanted to start fishing at once, for every second of my first visit to Redmire was so precious that I could not bear to waste just one. I gave Tony the first choice of swim, and he chose the 'Willows' which was close to the dam and had the reputation of being one of the best. I chose to fish to the right of the 'Oaks'. All the swims at Redmire had been named. I had read of these swims and of the carp that had been caught, so it seemed that I already knew them; they were like old friends. The lake, small and intimate and steeped in carp angling history seemed to be imbued with a special aura, anyone fishing at Redmire felt this atmosphere instinctively.

For some it must have felt awesome at first, and I'm sure Tony and I came under Redmire's spell for we found ourselves talking to each other in hushed tones. As for baits we both used standard Richworth boilies as marketed by Clive. We chose two flavours, Tutti Frutti and Salmon Supreme! Both had proved most successful on other waters so I started my swim baiting campaign immediately. We decided to introduce the baits into confined areas, rather than scattering them widely. This was on the advice of others who had fished the pool. It appeared such concentrations of bait were more likely to attract carp into the swim. The tackle rig I chose was the highly effective bolt rig. When a fish takes the bait and moves off drawing line through the eye of the weight it is brought up short by a back stop which prevents any more line being taken as the bead and stop jam up against the weight. This has the effect of making the hook prick the fish's mouth as it bolts off hence the name of the rig. As the fish tears off pulling the weight the resistance drives the hook in even further and the carp hooks itself. There are other refinements to make the resistance greater, but they would be difficult to describe in layman's terms and tedious for the non-angler to read.

The first day was pleasantly warm, with periods of sunshine. It was wonderfully relaxing by the pool, watching the play of light on the surface

and, through gaps between the trees on the opposite bank, the lush
unspoilt countryside. Now and again I wandered up to the shallows and
baited up another swim with particles. These were yet another bean called
boralloti, a health food product that I had caught carp on, and I knew that
they had been successful at Redmire in the past. As some time had elapsed
since anyone had fished with boralloti I hoped that the carp had forgotten
all about them. Back at the Oaks in the cool of the evening I caught a carp,
very small by Redmire standards, just a little 7-lb fish. It was a common
carp and I was delighted and encouraged, for it showed my exotic boilies
were likely to prove acceptable to the larger fish as well.

We fished at night, and even when we were so tired we just had to sleep,
we knew the bleeping of the Optonic Bite Alarm would instantly alert us.
The reserve swim in the shallows produced the odd carp for me, but they
were little fish; of the huge carp there was not a sign. By the close of the
second day the Willows had not lived up to its form at all, poor Tony had
not even had one twitch.

As is so predictable in an English summer, the weather changed for the
worse. A strong wind, almost a gale, funnelled down the little valley and
seemingly incessant rain drummed the surface of the pool as it poured out
of the sky. Redmire is normally renowned for its clarity, but after hours of
rain it became murky and full of colour, red as Devon soil, from all the
earth washed into the water. Even after the deluge ceased the weather
remained unsettled, with heavy intermittent showers sweeping in on the
westerly wind. As we fished on, catching nothing, we were still full of hope
for we knew that the great carp of Redmire were still there. We were not
too despondent either for we realized those fish would be difficult having
been fished for year after year by some of the finest anglers in the land.

All too soon Saturday evening arrived, and as we had to leave the
following morning we loaded the cars with non-essential equipment. By
this late stage with just one night's fishing left and an early morning
session to follow, even my enthusiasm was waning. On this particular
evening I had positioned the bait on the left hand rod so it lay close in to
the margins, under the oak branches that overhung the water. Indicator
bobbins of a new type called Monkey Climbers had become popular with
big fish anglers. They were an improvement on the bobbins that hung
down below the rod for this new variety could not be blown about in high
winds. The Monkey Climber as its name suggests could slide up and down
a thin metal rod which was pushed into the ground so that it remained
vertical. Furthermore when the carp rod was lifted from the rests to strike,

the bobbin automatically released the line. I was sitting on my bed chair keeping an eye on a steak I was cooking for the evening meal when I noticed the bobbin on the left hand rod slowly inching upward. My first reaction was to think that the bobbin was moving in response to a 'line bite'. This occurs if a fish bumps into or touches the line. Then it dawned on me that this could not possibly be so as the line was lying on the bottom of the pool. Carefully I eased myself off the chair, taking care not to kick over the Gaz stove. Just as I was about to grasp the rod the handle of the reel started to revolve, what carp anglers call 'churning'. The bolt rig had worked and the churn told me a carp was leaving the margin as fast as it could. Striking gently in case the hook was not fully embedded, I imagined by the feel of the line and the bend in the rod that I had hooked yet another small fish. Tony, who was fishing not so far away, politely enquired whether I needed help, I replied that he might just as well not bother as it was only a little fish. That carp was soon close in again, below the tip of my rod, then suddenly realising that it could be in trouble, it wrenched the rod down and tore off towards the middle of the pool. It was now obvious that I was connected to a sizeable fish. Redmire carp have rather softer mouth tissue than carp from most waters, so I handled that fish with extra care. At last after many an anxious moment the carp was guided across the front of the net and sank down safely into the folds. The fish was a fine mirror carp just three ounces over twenty pounds.

Realizing I had been incorrect in my original estimate of the carp's size, Tony had arrived while I was playing it, and seeing the neglected, and by now smouldering steak, turned off the stove while we weighed and photographed the fish and returned it to the water. A Tutti Frutti boilie had led to that carp's downfall, so re-baiting with another, I cast it under the trees in exactly the same place as before.

I was trying to make something of the steak—even burnt offerings can be palatable when eaten in the open air, as those who have suffered garden barbecues on a cold, draughty summer evening can testify—when the unexpected happened. The bobbin rose up the monkey needle and striking far more smartly than on the first occasion I hooked a second carp. This was a good fish of a size with the first, but a smooth-flanked leather carp rather than one of the more numerous mirrors and commons. It was an unusual colour and Tony said it was a well-known fish that had been caught before by the regular syndicate members and nicknamed 'Raspberry' because of its overall pink hue. Raspberry weighed 22 lb 6 oz.

The rest of the night passed without incident and predictably the

following morning was warm and sunny, foretelling better weather to come which is par for the course when fishing trips have to be planned in advance. With all the gear stowed away we drove up the hill pausing on the crest to look back wistfully. Redmire glistened in the sunlight and we thought of its huge carp preparing to bask undisturbed as the sun, now high in the sky, blazed down on that secluded valley. I was fortunate in catching two 'twenties' on my first visit to Redmire, for Tony, using the same baits and experienced in the ways of carp as he undoubtedly was, had failed to get a bite. It often happens—when anglers of equal experience, using identical tackle, identical baits, fish the same area of water, one will catch, the other won't—there's no logical reason why this should occur, but it happens time and time again.

The best of anglers have blank days. If this were not so the catching of fish would become so predictable as to eventually become a bore. After a lifetime's fishing there's always so much yet to learn, new challenges beckon and rarely do the best-laid plans work out as expected. Perhaps it is just these unpredictable aspects of angling that cause so many to indulge in this fascinating sport.

Not long after this first and two subsequent visits to Redmire, news was filtering through the grapevine of a lake situated in southern France that contained enormous carp. This water, Lake Cassien near Cannes was huge, at least 4,000 acres in extent. A few adventurous English anglers notably Rod Hutchinson, Max Cottis and Paul Regent had, it was rumoured, caught some magnificent carp. Living in so much warmer a climate than the carp in English waters, the fish of Cassien could feed and grow for at least nine months of the year. Even the three winter months were normally mild and such conditions suited the carp so well that they grew to phenomenal size. Few anglers knew of Cassien until Paul Regent started to organise coach trips to the lake, with night accommodation arranged for anglers in Cannes. Night fishing was illegal so this was a sensible arrangement, the lake could be fished all day, then the short journey to Cannes allowed the anglers to relax and sample any number of restaurants. Gradually the anglers making the long journey south came to know the best areas of the lake for carp fishing, the depths, and the kind of tackle not only to combat the snaggy bottom, but also to handle fish far greater in size than they had caught before.

The grapevine really buzzed when Max Cottis caught a 68-lb carp. I suppose some were sceptical of such a report unaware that carp could be so huge, but their doubts were dispelled when pictures of the great fish were blazoned on the front pages of the angling press. Such an event really set the carp world alight. Further reports of other big carp began to appear at regular intervals and as I read each one I realized that I too would not rest until I was sitting beside my rods on the shore of Cassien. Hang the distance, hang the expense, I was determined to get to the south of France come what may! Derrick Amies, his son Jason, Andy Barker a tackle dealer with a business in Coventry and I, started to plan an assault on Cassien's carp.

Late August to early September was the only feasible time that any of us could spare two weeks from our respective business commitments. We hoped to allow for ten days at the water, plus two days for the journey both ways. As Cassien is a thousand miles from Norfolk we realized that we should have to drive all the way, with only short stops for essentials such as fuel. We crossed to the Continent on the 8.30 p.m. ferry to Calais, and after clearing customs set off for Paris where we joined the fast *auto route* to Lyons and onward to Marseilles. By dawn we had left Lyons behind, and by taking turns at the wheel so no-one became overtired we sped on steadily. It was a sensible arrangement for continuous driving on French roads is beyond the average driver. At Les Everettes junction we turned off onto the country road that led to the lake.

Everyone was wide awake and keen to catch the first glimpse of Cassien. It was a boiling hot day and when we saw the West Arm, some of the South Arm and eventually the huge expanse of the North Arm, sparkling azure blue, we could hardly believe our eyes. It seemed, after the tiny waters that we were used to fishing in England, that we were gazing on an inland sea. Jason, full of youthful enthusiasm, wanted to start fishing at once but keen as we all were we prudently decided to visit the Anglers Tourist Guide at Chez Pierre Cafe. We were greeted warmly and after so tiring a journey we were glad to sit down to a leisurely *petit dejeuner* on the shady veranda. Afterwards, we obtained our fishing permits, being reminded that we must not attempt to fish at night, then arranged to hire a boat. The boat cost £10 per day, an unavoidable expense as a boat was the only means of reaching much of the shoreline which was inaccessible by car. We didn't fancy long treks in such wild country where rumour had it that a certain spider's bite could be lethal and the odd wild boar was apt to roam. Perhaps the most important reason for having a boat was its use as a platform from which to play big fish. We knew if one of us hooked the huge Cassien carp it would be unstoppable at first, stripping yard after yard of line from the reel. As the lake bed was littered with tree stumps,

drowned bushes and heaven knows what else, if you didn't follow the fish by boat, it was almost certain that the line would become snagged in an obstruction.

My friend Clive Diedrich, who had been at Cassien for two weeks just prior to our arrival had told us of such problems and was also generous enough to tell us where the carp might be located. Without such up-to-date information we should have been at a loss to know where to start fishing with such a vast area of water to contend with. So, having been advised that a fair number of carp were in the South Arm, we decided that we could do no better than make a start there. We discovered two small islands, and immediately felt that we should fish from these. Islands in English carp waters always seem to attract carp and we thought such features might have the same influence with the carp of Cassien. It is always important to choose a swim to fish for a reason, so often anglers just settle down in the first comfortable place they come across. Having a reason for choosing a swim automatically imbues the angler with confidence and as I said earlier, confident anglers catch fish.

We had brought along our echo sounder, so having ferried all the gear over to the islands we quietly rowed around discovering the depth of water and of course any horrendous snags. Some twenty yards offshore there was a depth of some fifteen feet then the bottom fell away quickly, at maximum casting range it was very deep—fifty-five feet. Derrick and his son chose one of the islands while Andy and I shared the other.

We had no means of knowing what depth the carp preferred, so to cover as much of the water as possible we set up three rods each—all were 12-foot long, powerful carp rods, matched to 15-lb breaking strain line. One bait was cast to the 15-20 feet contour, one far out in the deeps and the last one between these two extremes. Such tactics we thought would cover most eventualities. We had brought along thousands of deep-frozen boilies, transported in cool boxes. I pre-baited the swim with at least three thousand, which sounds perhaps over generous, but I felt that such a number might be needed to attract carp in such a large deep lake. I also thought that such a concentration of baits would inevitably interest any carp passing by the islands. On reflection I think I was mistaken, with so many free offerings the odds of a carp taking the hook bait among hundreds of others were very long indeed. It would be rather like searching for the proverbial needle.

With the bottom such a minefield of snags, in addition to the extra strong line we had hooks that were much larger and stronger than we would ever use back home, where small hooks were and still are much favoured by carp anglers. Our bombs, also heavy, were necessary when using the bolt rig at long range. Carp are wary of picking up a bait with the line leading directly from it, so we used the hair or rather two, one tied to the hook eye the other to the bend. Each hair contained three baits with the six baits nicely concentrated. We hoped our baits would be visible and perhaps distinctive among the mass of free samples. That first afternoon soon passed and only when the echo sounding, pre-baiting and setting up the tackle had been completed could we find time to enjoy our surroundings.

Cassien is set in a leisure park, and is popular not only with the French but other Europeans. What with camp sites, the crowds, not to mention boaters and bathers, certain parts of the lake shore can become crowded. But the lake is so big with much of it without road access, anglers can get far away from disturbance. The shore is dry and sandy, the hillsides densely wooded and the water is wonderfully clear; at the time of our visit the lake always reflected the blue Mediterranean sky. The next day we were ready to start fishing at sunrise, 5.30 am. Then it was pleasantly warm, but before long the temperature rose steadily to reach a sweltering 100 °F. Derrick, Jason and Andy decided to row back to the cafe, mainly to purchase a large supply of drinks for we realized that a full day in such tropical conditions could leave us seriously dehydrated. However, they also hoped to discover news of where any carp had been caught and generally to pick up any information that might prove useful. I remained so as to watch over our tackle, and Andy's rods with their baits still in the water. Because of the rough nature of the lake beds the rods were angled upward in the rests so as to keep at least some of the line off the bottom. The effect of the heat was soporofic. I still had not fully recovered after the hours of driving so, with the sun beating down upon a lake surface motionless as a sheet of glass, and convinced that in such conditions there was little chance of catching anything, I fell into that twilight between sleep and wakefulness.

As if in a dream, I heard an irritating high-pitched continuous note. Awake but bemused I glanced at my three rods. The optonic bite alarm bleeps on the left-hand indicator had merged into one continuous urgent note. Line was pouring off the reel spool, I leapt up, grabbed the rod and holding it as high as possible to keep the line clear of snags, set the hook. The rod bent and already at least 100 yards of line had been taken from the reel. I could not use the boat alone, so I had no option but to play the fish from the island hoping against hope that the line would remain free. Slowly I pumped the fish nearer. Pumping is a technique for gaining line back onto the reel. The rod is raised toward the vertical then lowered, during the lowering process a yard or two of line can be recovered but line tension must be maintained at all times.

Slowly and with infinite care I worked the carp ever closer until at last I could see its shadowy form beneath the surface, then it was all over. With the fish safely in the landing net I lifted it ashore. Parting the folds of the net I beheld my first Cassien carp. It was a superb fish in pristine condition and I doubt if it had been caught before. At 27 lb 12 oz it was a large carp by normal standards, but perhaps unexceptional for Cassein. But it had fought as no other carp I had caught ever had, I was elated. I put the fish in the black nylon keep sack where it could remain quiet and regain its strength. Now keenly alert, I re-baited, cast out and awaited the return of the others. My fish was greeted with enthusiasm and after the photographs had been taken it was released, and because the water was so clear we followed its course as it glided off heading for deep water.

Soon a number of large carp were rolling and splashing over the area where Andy's baits were positioned. They were obviously interested in the mass of baits that littered the bottom. We expected Andy to get a bite at any second but as the minutes, then the hours passed the optonics remained obstinately silent. We certainly expected more carp activity in the cool of the evening but all our baits remained untouched.

The next day was as hot as the first, the others once again decided the return to Chez Pierre but I hadn't journeyed 1,000 miles just to relax and socialise when I could be fishing for perhaps some of the largest carp in the world. So I remained by the rods enjoying the wide vista of wild countryside and always full of hope that a great carp would fancy one of my baits. When the heat seemed at its most intense, close on mid-day, I had another fast run with the line hissing through the rod rings. Once again the line remained clear of obstructions and I landed another carp of 23 lb 8 oz.

During the afternoon young Jason hooked a fish which he played skilfully. When he had coaxed the fish close to the bank for some inexplicable reason the hook hold gave way and the carp gained its freedom. Jason was bitterly disappointed. At first we had expected, if we were going to catch carp at all, that our best chance would be in the morning or evening, not during the stifling daytime heat. But Cassien's carp did not appear to behave like their English counterparts. There did not seem to be any regular feeding pattern, bites could come at any time.

Later I had yet another run; why my baits were taken and not those of the others, fishing in the same area with identical tackle and baits remains a mystery. It must have been frustrating for those who remained fishless. By the time I had moved the few feet to the rod the reel spool was half empty. It was a hectic, struggling battle and I was sweating, drained of energy before Andy skilfully slipped the wide landing net under the fish. It was my largest carp and pulled the needle of the scales down to register 32 lb 8 oz. Tiredness forgotten, I returned to my chair content; at that moment I felt that I should not mind if I never had another bite for the remainder of our stay.

Because few fish if any appeared to favour Derrick and Jason's island they asked if they could join us on ours. As there was plenty of room we agreed. This proved to be an excellent arrangement as we could spend the long hot hours between carp runs discussing ideas to improve our chances. Everyone had opinions and the time seemed to pass more quickly as we tried to find the solution to the problem of increasing our catch rate. Now the carp seemed to change their feeding times and most rolling and similar activities occurred both in the morning and the evening. We did not have another bite that day. We fished through the heat of the following day and at long last around mid-day once again, one of Derrick's baits was taken. All went well and eventually he landed a stupendous fish of 36 lb 8 oz. It certainly made the long fishless days worthwhile and we were delighted. That fish was the largest Derrick had ever caught and was to be the best of the holiday.

Jason, not wanting to be outdone by his father landed a carp too, his first, a 'twenty' plus another pound and a half. He was a very happy young man and it was a joy to see his grinning face. Now only Andy was fishless, but in spite of this he seemed to remain remarkably cheerful and optimistic under the circumstances. After the next day had passed and not one of us had had a bite I felt we should move; everyone agreed.

The shore below the road that followed the contour of the South Arm looked promising. Here the water was shallow for Cassien, a long cast might just reach a depth of twenty-five feet. A quick survey led to the discovery of a small peninsula, and from this vantage point it was possible to cast out to the twenty-five foot contour, as well as cover much shallower water closer in. Fishing from a point that juts out into a lake has one important advantage. Fish cruising along the shoreline have to pass around the tip of the peninsula, and often they pass by within easy casting

Jason Amies with a 21lb 8-oz Cassien carp.

range. They seem to follow one particular route as if it were a familiar piscine highway.

Our pre-baiting was not so generous, perhaps five hundred baits or so, and we positioned these exactly by using the boat. In no time I caught a twelve and a half pounder. This raised our spirits and Andy's enthusiasm after witnessing this event was heartening. After an hour or so, I felt that a walk to the cafe would give me some much needed exercise. I left my three rods on the rests with the baits where I had cast them and asked Andy to take charge of them for me. When I returned I didn't have to be told the good news, for as I approached I could tell by the smirk on Andy's countenance that he had caught a carp.

The peninsula was proving to be a good swim and that evening both Andy and I hooked fish that were far, far larger than any fish we had landed to date. But on each occasion the line became impossibly jammed in the tangle of tree stumps that littered the bed of the lake in the vicinity of the point. We had planned that this was to be our last day but encouraged by hooking these very large fish we decided to remain for a further twenty-four hours.

I decided to keep on the move on this final day, fishing a number of swims on the off chance that I might by some miracle find a real 'hot spot' and hook a monster fish. Also, being mobile gave me a chance to reconnoitre new swims in preparation for another time. Not one of us was successful that day but during the holiday, Derrick, Jason and I had landed our biggest carp and we were content.

It was not until 1987 that we could fish Lake Cassien again. Derrick and I had become so deeply involved in our Norwich Angling Centre, often working long hours, that finding the time to go fishing was virtually impossible. Retail angling shops are not too busy in the close season so that was the only time of the year that we could be away for any length of time. We decided that some time in May, just after the Cassien carp had spawned, would perhaps be the best time to locate them.

Derrick took Jason as before and this time my son Neil accompanied me. In the meantime Andy had fished Cassien and been rewarded with a huge 60-lb fish; he deserved it. For the last few years the Norfolk springs had been bitterly cold and we were looking forward to some respite from such unpleasant weather by basking in the warmth of southern France. Apart from a torrential rain storm just after we left Paris the journey passed without incident. On arrival at Cassien, although the sky was overcast it was so much warmer than chilly East Anglia where biting north-east winds can make early summers a misery. Driving along beside the South Arm to see if there were any other anglers we found the shoreline deserted. At Chez Pierre, where our greeting was as friendly as ever, we asked question after question concerning our chances of contacting the really big fish—which area of the lake we should concentrate on— and of course had anyone been fishing lately. As far as we could ascertain two Dutch anglers had been fishing for nearly a month! Our confidence soared when we were told that one of them had caught an enormous 74-lb carp. Leaving Jason and Neil to sort out the 25,000 baits and store them in the cafe's huge freezer Derrick and I decided to survey the West Arm. We discovered the Dutchmen fishing the shallows at the very top. In spite of having taken so magnificent a fish, they had caught little else. I noticed carp activity in the next bay to the Dutch and it was there we decided to make a start.

On this occasion we hired one of the foot-operated paddle boats, because they appeared more stable than those propelled by oars and were fitted with a platform at the bow. This platform provided a safe and sure foothold and it looked as if it would be easier to play a fish from such a vantage point rather than from the less stable rowing boat. Jason and Neil had the unenviable task of paddling the one and half miles to the bay; they stuck to the job manfully but were both very hot and weary by the time they arrived.

The West Arm is quite narrow, winding between densely wooded banks. Although deep in parts, there were extensive shallows in the 15–25-foot range which we imagined would be the depth that carp might prefer. We fished for some hours without incident, then pre-baited ready for an early start on the following day. We had modified our tackle as a direct result of our first visit. It seemed wherever we fished we just could not avoid the ever present tree stumps and bottom debris. In an attempt to circumvent these we used fluted bombs which when reeled in quickly tended to plane upwards, and to keep as much of the line off the bottom when actually fishing we used a free-running controller on the line. This was a small elongated balsa wood float with a hole bored through its length. Being so light this did not follow the bomb when cast, but hung back due to air pressure. The distance from tackle rig to controller could be regulated by a sliding knot tied to the line which acted as a backstop; during the cast this prevented the controller sliding back too far. Being buoyant the controller supported much of the line keeping it off the bottom.

Dad posing with Neil Plummer's 36lb 14-oz Cassien carp.

A 41¹/2-lb Cassien carp.

Otherwise our tackle was as before, and we still used our six baits, three to a hair connected to the hook. This time we had brought some buoyant boilies or 'pop ups' which we baited on each alternate rod. This allowed us to present the baits so they floated a few inches above the bottom. Pop ups are of course even more visible than baits lying on the bottom and have accounted for many a large carp in English waters.

Our first day at Cassien started with a blustery wind, clouds raced across the sky but periods of sunshine alternated with the showers. By mid-day the breaks in the cloud became more frequent, the wind eased and it became pleasantly warm. Hours passed, without one of us getting a carp run, but it was early days and it was such a change to bask in the sun that no-one seemed concerned.

Our tranquillity was interrupted by an English voice. Unnoticed, a coach had stopped on the road behind us, this contained twenty-seven carp anglers led by Kevin Maddocks, a publisher and fine carp angler. There was little we could tell them apart from the one great fish caught by the Dutchmen. With this unexpected influx of anglers, and no doubt much bustle and activity to come we decided to leave for more peaceful surroundings. Transferring to the South Arm, pre-baiting swims and moving to a new one every second day, including those we had fished on our previous visit, we fished on hour after hour from dawn to dusk. In four whole days no one had a bite! However, on the fifth day Derrick who had already decided to move and fish right at the extremity of the Arm, hooked and lost a carp. Later on I had one of those sizzling runs where the line blurs as it pours off the reel. I was urged to take to the boat but before I could reach it, the fish kited to my left and in spite of the controller the line jammed solid. How I cursed those infernal snags. The Dacron hook length had snapped. After so many blank days this was a terrible blow the more so because it was certain that I had lost a very large carp indeed.

Our failure was not peculiar to us alone, on one of our periodic visits to the cafe we discovered that the party of English anglers were finding things quite as difficult as we were, which was I suppose some consolation.

Neil and I moved yet again to a peninsula situated half way along the Arm. By now, keen angler that I am, I had begun to convince myself that nobody was likely to catch anything. I began to wonder if the carp were miles away, perhaps they were shoaled up in the deeps, or up the North Arm, and I became more and more despondent.

We loaded up the boat and paddled towards the peninsula. As we approached I saw a carp roll, not twenty yards off the point. How my spirits rose. So as not to disturb any carp we eased the boat ashore then towed it quietly along the margin. As we were preparing to set up our tackle some more carp rolled. Frantically we put some baits into the swim, set up the rods, cast out both bottom and pop up baits, and full of anticipation, awaited a bite which we expected any minute.

I had thoroughly learnt the lesson that any attempt to play carp from the bank was almost certain to result in the line fouling a tree stump, so the boat was beached close by with the landing net aboard, so that if I did hook a fish I could leap in and head for deep water. We felt that after all our efforts we really did deserve to catch something better than the two tench which were the only fish we had caught, a day or two earlier. At least Jason's was a fine 7-lb fish, mine was considerably smaller. I had told Neil that if a carp did take one of the baits on my rods he could do the honours. In spite of the carp activity that we had seen on our arrival, we had been sitting for possibly two hours, with the optonics mute and the Monkey Climber bobbins immobile. Then what I was again convinced was highly unlikely happened at last. One of my baits had been taken, and as line left the reel spool at an alarming rate, we rushed to the boat. I held the rod high, and Neil paddled like one demented until we were in deep water two hundred yards off shore. I handed the rod over to Neil. He reeled in line until he felt the weight of the fish, and slamming the rod back over his shoulder set the hook. I doubted if this was necessary as I was certain the heavy bomb allied to the bolt rig had resulted in the carp hooking itself. It took Neil all of twenty minutes to pump the carp up from the bottom eighty-five feet down. The fish looked beaten but I had difficulty in reaching it with the net as the boat kept drifting away. With one inelegant swoop I managed to get at least half the carp into the net. With a last burst of furious energy the carp bolted downward with such force that the handle of the net broke. This was a predicament we had not bargained for. In spite of his aching arms, Neil inched the fish to the surface, and even with the handicap of the broken handle, made rather a better job of netting it. Neil had done his work superbly and thoroughly deserved his 36 lb 14-oz fish.

Carp were still attracted by our baits off the peninsula for while we were fighting Neil's fish I heard some heavy splashes which seemed to come from that area. Back on shore, the fish weighed, photographed and returned to the water, we renewed the baits and wondered if we would be fortunate enough to hook another carp. I had a fast run, struck and felt nothing; the afternoon slipped away. One of my baits positioned only

Andy Barker of Coventry nets a 36$\frac{1}{2}$-lb Cassien carp for Derrick Amies.

some twenty yards away was taken and once more we rushed to the boat. As this was our last day Neil had been making the boat tidy and shipshape, we had hardly paddled a few yards before I realized that the net had been left behind. Neil had laid it aside while cleaning out the boat. Neil didn't hesitate, slipped over the side, swam and waded ashore, grabbed the net, and returning heaved into the boat. There just wasn't time to help him aboard, indeed with me being fully engaged in playing a carp it would have been foolhardy. By now the situation was becoming ludicrous, I was paddling the boat, trying to steer in the right direction and deal with a heavy powerful fish as well. Somehow I reached the deep water and was able to gain the bow platform and handle the fish in a more competent manner. It was at least twenty-five minutes before I saw the fish circling in the clear water below the boat. In spite of the handicap of a broken net, I made a more professional job, soon boated the carp and headed for shore.

This fish seemed shorter than Neil's and I guessed its weight would be in the high thirties. It was a mirror carp; with just one row of huge scales along its flanks, this type is known as a linear mirror—the usual scale arrangement of a mirror carp is far more haphazard with no two fish alike. We were amazed that this magnificent-looking fish scaled 41 lb 8 oz.

On this our last day I had arranged to meet up with the others at Chez Pierre at 6.30 pm. I saw Derrick's boat in the distance heading towards the cafe. Loathe to leave, we stowed the gear and paddled off. When we met them neither had seen hide nor hair of a fish. But they were pleased we had succeeded and it was a fine excuse to celebrate in Cannes that evening, where we found room in a restaurant in spite of the overcrowding—the Cannes Film Festival was in full swing. We enjoyed the wine, toasts were drunk to this and that, but above all to the great carp of Lake Cassien and of course 'to the next time'.

So far the largest carp caught by an English angler from this beautiful lake weighed 77 lb. One can hardly conceive of a carp so huge, and no doubt before long someone will break the 80-lb barrier. No-one knows for certain just how big a carp can become, but there is perhaps the possibility that a 100-lb carp could be cruising the crystal depths of Lake Cassien.

What of other lakes abroad, and the huge carp that may lurk in them? Already English carp anglers have journeyed to eastern European countries in search of a leviathan. The carp anglers of England have developed the tackle, skills and techniques that have amazed anglers in other lands. Perhaps one day their exploits will be hailed as the greatest angling adventure of all.

Tench: The Summer Fish of Misty Dawns

Olive green, dusky brown or occasionally black as ink with creamy-coloured undersides, sometimes pink or orange tinged, tench are traditionally sought by the angler in high summer.

Hidden in the mists of early dawn the fisherman crouches beside age-old lakes and weed-choked waters where great rafts of water lilies, shady and cool, shelter the tench which glide indolently below. So akin in colour to their environment as to be nearly invisible, except for their tiny jewel-like, ruby-red eyes, tench are a pure complement to the dark-toned greens of their underwater jungle.

But at dawn, in the cool of the evening or when the sky is overcast and light values are low, the tench forage hard, thrusting their heads deep into the bottom silt, seeking for midge larvae, the rich red bloodworm. As they sift through the mud, streams of tiny bubbles rise, passing out through their gill covers to froth at the surface. By such signs the tench unwittingly disclose their whereabouts and as the patterns of bubbles rise, disperse and are renewed, the tench angler feels his pulse quicken as he gently casts his bait so that his float lies still, close by the bubble clusters.

Those who have never smelt the pure freshness of a June morning as day dawns and the mist smokes from the glassy surface of the lake, have missed a rare pleasure indeed. Unlike the sharp purity of mountain air, or the heady ozone by the seashore, the atmosphere of an ancient lake has a unique misty quality. The scent of mud and water-weeds, sometimes so all-pervading is softened and subtly mixed with the smell of new-mown hay and the sweet, pungent tang of water mint. At this time of day only nature is fully awake and in the stillness only the soporific, melodious cooing of wood pigeons, the little splashes as tiny fish flip at the surface, and the unexpected, sharp, staccato cry of a moorhen disturb the tranquillity.

The bankside vegetation is now in full leaf—the trees are clothed in bright pristine greens and the yellow flower heads of flag iris, standing like sentinels at the water's edge spear the air. As the sun climbs and the dew gives its last sparkle before evaporating in the increasing warmth, the reed warblers chatter incessantly, flitting from reed stem to reed stem. The droning of innumerable insects is overlaid by the busy hum of bumble-bees searching for their first sips of nectar from the clusters of cream and pink clover. The tench angler, intently watching his float, whose richly-coloured tip will hopefully sink from sight, cannot be immune to the lush fecundity of his surroundings. By stealing a few precious hours from the tedium and pressures of everyday life he can relax and be at peace.

Tench, once bred in stewponds along with carp to grace monastic tables, are a hardy and successful species able to thrive in conditions lethal to other fish: from clouded muddy ponds to slow meandering rivers; from weed-choked lakes to recently-excavated gravel pits. This hardy fish is most numerous in southern counties, but many a Yorkshire water and the Cheshire meres seem to suit them too—there are even a handful in the waters of the Scottish lowlands.

Covered in scales so tiny that its body appears velvet smooth, the tench's appearance serves to camouflage its great strength and muscular form so that anglers have learnt to respect its sustained power and instinct for the shortest route to tackle-snatching snags. The tench is thickset; the wrist of the tail (unlike other fish) only narrows slightly before sprouting a huge black paintbrush of a tail, wherein lies its swimming power. Tench fight hard when hooked, thumping the bent rod in a series of wrenching pulls. The more pressure the angler applies, the harder the tench responds; they are doughty adversaries.

Male tench are smaller than their mates, but because they are endowed with even greater tails and enlarged ventral fins they can surprise the inexperienced fisherman, who can be misled into imagining that he has hooked a far heavier fish. Male tench fight as hard as any fish that swim our waters.

Not so long ago anyone who landed a 5-lb tench was justly proud, and for a long time the largest—just one—that had even been caught on rod and line was a little over 7 lb in weight. But in June 1987 the once unattainable 10-lb barrier was smashed when an enormous tench of 14 lb 5 oz was hooked and landed in the large gravel pit at Wraysbury. It is interesting to speculate why if such vast tench have existed in other waters, have tench been caught in the last decade that are far larger then ever before?

I can only theorise but I think two factors are responsible. High nutritional value baits, full of protein, can result in fish putting on weight faster and hence growing larger than if they had to rely on natural food.

Tench are notorious for becoming preoccupied with one food type when it is abundant, so once they discovered hundreds of the high protein 'boilies' littering the bottom, put in by many carp anglers, they fed on them avidly. Secondly, and perhaps not quite so important a reason, is that with contemporary tackle, baits can be cast long distances undreamed of by anglers before the advent of the fixed spool reel.

Such events were far in the future when as a youngster I tried my hand at tench fishing. Tactics to catch tench were traditional and time honoured as were the times of day that they could be expected to feed. The latter has never changed with regard to the small ponds and lakes but tench in the larger gravel pits have taken to patrolling the margins and gravel bars throughout the day, and they are not averse to picking up any baits they encounter on their travels.

I was 15 years old when, under the guidance of my father and by listening to the advice of the other helpful and tolerant club members I was fast becoming an angler. This was no boyhood whim. Unlike many other boys who occasionally went fishing when there was nothing better to do, I spent all my spare time at the waterside looking, learning and gaining experience. Tench fishing was new to me and I was fired with enthusiasm.

The Bradford City Angling Club controlled a large pond or little lake; it could rightly be described as either. Shipton Lake was a typical tench water set among sheltering trees and some eight feet deep in the deepest part. The bottom was covered in soft water-weeds—particularly in the shallower water—and the lake bed consisted of soft mud that nurtured the roots of the yellow-flowered common water lily. Their leaves, green oblong discs floating on the surface, extended from the margins where the wild flag iris grew in abundance. Where the bottom was less muddy, the thin tubular stems of the true bullrush stood in serried ranks. Shipton Lake was a beautiful place, an oasis of peace after the never ending hustle and bustle of grimy Rotherham. This little water could be fished by obtaining a day permit from Bradford City Angling Club. During the summer the Rotherham club which I had joined, took coach parties to the Yorkshire Ouse dropping off those who wanted to fish at Shipton on the way to the river. Because we did not reach the lake early enough I missed some of the best fishing, just after dawn, but I was usually fishing from eight o'clock with the knowledge that at least I could look forward to tench activity in the evening.

I caught the Shipton tench by float fishing using 4-lb breaking strain line tied to a relatively small but strong number 8 hook. I also used a special

method of float fishing called the 'lift'. This deadly way of catching tench had only just been introduced, and few tench anglers were aware of the method. Everyone, angler or not, knows that when a fish takes the bait the float submerges. But when lift fishing the opposite occurs, the float rises then falls flat on the surface, that is if the angler doesn't strike first. While the lift method is remarkably efficient it is limited in that it can only be used in water of less depth than the length of the rod, and also when the water is still and calm. You may wonder how the float can rise up when a fish bites, surely it must pull it under? The secret lay in the way in which the float was attached to the line and where the anchoring split shot was situated. Normally, enough shot are nipped on the line so as to make the float sit in the water vertically but in the lift method only one large shot is used. This is nipped on the line quite near the hook even as close as two inches from it, but certainly no more than six. This single shot must be just heavy enough to submerge the float unless the shot is resting on the bottom. In other words the weight slowly pulls the float down. The angler uses his float as a bite indicator and needs to see its brightly coloured tip, so the distance between the shot and float has to be adjusted so that the tip protrudes from the surface. Having plumbed the depth, the distance from shot to float is arranged to be ever so slightly more than the depth of water. Now with the shot anchoring the float, which incidentally must be fixed to the line at its base only, the float will lie flat. If the angler reels in slowly, as the line tightens to the shot the float will cock into the vertical position but angled slightly towards the rod.

As the line tension to hold the float in such a position is critical the rod cannot be held, but is positioned in two rod rests, its tip pointing at the float. So sensitive is this method that by turning the reel handle and tightening the line the float tip can be made to sink lower until only a fraction is above the surface. Of course even if you understand the principle of how to set the float, the question why it rises when a fish bites has still to be resolved. If you remember the anchoring shot was close to the hook. A tench feeds by upending, head down, then having obtained a mouthful of food reverts to the horizontal. Because the shot is so near to the hook, this latter movement on the part of the tench lifts the shot clear of the bottom. The float, now no longer anchored falls flat, but before it can do so its buoyancy causes it to rise before becoming unstable and falling over.

The lift method of float fishing is a delicate and supremely efficient way of catching wary tench in hard-fished waters. So I fished thus, with the float drawn close by lily pads, groundbaiting with balls of moistened breadcrumbs and pieces of worm. For bait I put my faith in garden worms which anglers call 'lobs'; effective they were too and I soon became proficient at catching what were really quite small fish; rarely did one weigh more than 4 lb. But for a young lad of fifteen these were long awaited and exciting times and I learnt much about the habits of tench and how best to catch them. The method other anglers used at Shipton was to freeline a bait. This is the simplest method of all, no weights or float just a hook tied to the line. The bait is cast out—obviously distance is limited—and allowed to sink, slowly, enticingly, to rest gently on the bottom. Sometimes the worm was dispensed with and replaced with pieces of fluffy new white bread, 'flake' in anglers' terms. I used this freeline method too, to some effect.

I needed worms for my tench fishing, lots of them, and digging the garden was not only hard work, but became less and less productive as I eroded their numbers. Anglers know how to get half a bucket of large healthy lobworms with the minimum of effort. The essentials are a warm night, soon after rain or even better if rain is falling. Then on lawns, sports grounds or parks, wherever there is short mown grass, the worms appear on the surface. Worms do not generally surface until after midnight and retreat down their holes as night fades. There's truth in the saying 'the early bird catches the worm' but then few are aware that so does the angler, creeping across the grass in the dead of night!

There's an art in worm catching. The first requirement is a dim torch (one whose bulb has been masked with red paper is excellent—shine a light directly onto a worm and it retreats down its hole like lightning). Next, is stealth; any undue vibration has the same effect on a worm as a bright light. When conditions are suitable the worms emerge, lying full length on the damp grass but always with their tailends still in the hole, so they can retreat in a flash if danger threatens.

It takes practise to spot a worm in dim red light and even more to differentiate between head and tail. But the head end is blue grey and slightly irridescent while the tail is more flat in section and is a pale translucent pink. Having found a worm its escape route must be blocked and this is easily achieved by pinning the tail to the ground, pressing down firmly with a finger. Then the other hand holds the worm and pulls gently. While only the tip of the tail is anchored in the hole it is surprising the amount of muscular power a worm can exert, and it needs some seconds of steady pulling to make it release its grip. Pull too hard and the worm will

break in half; as I said worm catching is an art!

Once I obtained my own transport—the first was a motor cycle combination—I no longer had to rely on the bus, train or organised coach outings. This immediately widened my horizons, not only could I travel to new waters but I could arrive so that I could be fishing as the day dawned.

I began to visit Langold Lake which was near Worksop. This was a larger water reputed to hold some better sized fish and was chock full of tench. Langold was subject to prolific summer weed growth, particularly around the margins but there were specially constructed fishing platforms which helped mitigate the problem. It was a natural lake, with a depth of seven to eight feet of water at the dam end. It was a popular place, and not only with anglers, having a lido and swimming pool. Some people actually swam in the lake itself, so because of such disturbances it was necessary to fish early or late. Certainly the tench were of a better size and I spent many a magic summer dawn watching with bated breath as the tench bubbles erupted at the surface close by my float. I remember one local angler getting a 5-lb tench though I doubt if there were many of these or even if bigger fish were present.

So keen was I to catch a large tench that I tried a number of Yorkshire waters, some of them far from Rotherham. I caught plenty of fish but a really large one eluded me.

Reports began to filter through the grapevine of a lake in Norfolk that was producing what were considered at that time very large tench indeed. The specimen hunting grapevine for those plugged into the service is usually accurate. Somehow, in spite of much secrecy the news of a water producing large fish does not remain a secret for long. It only takes a few long distance phone calls and every big fish angler has acquired at least some of the facts.

This water had been given a name by those few Norfolk anglers fishing there, 'the Marsh'. This made it quite difficult to pinpoint but I knew roughly where the lake was situated, so it was a simple matter spending a few minutes searching for a lake on the Ordnance Survey map of the area to be pretty certain I had located it.

This was in the mid-Seventies when tench as large as six and seven pounds were considered fish of a lifetime. Tench fishing techniques had advanced, special fast taper rods for long distance fishing could be obtained and a number of tench anglers formed the 'Tench Fishers'. These comparatively few experienced anglers willingly shared their knowledge with each other and undoubtedly more and more really large tench were being caught by design and not by accident. Apart from the well proven traditional baits such as bread, worms or maggots anglers found tench were extremely fond of sweetcorn. Certainly pre-baiting was essential, but once the tench discovered sweetcorn was good to eat it became a popular bait.

The Marsh is a shallow, weedy lake, some seven acres in extent, set in ancient parkland not far from Aylsham. The banks are low lying and open but this unusual terrain for an ancestral lake is due to cattle being able to graze the bankside vegetation. However, there are fine trees, particularly oaks by the lake, whose slightly open quality is further relieved by an island and boathouse.

Once I had found the house, for the lake cannot be discerned from the lane, I discovered an old exercise book in an outhouse. In this book you were required to write your name and address, leaving the modest fee in an open box. It was obvious that the owners trusted the local anglers implicitly, for the box contained a scattering of notes and coins, apparently only rarely collected.

The path to the lake led beside the old walled vegetable garden,

A perfect tench lake in Norfolk; the spot where I made my tench
film.

alongside the tennis court and after passing through a small shrubbery a gate opened into a meadow. Horses grazed here, and there was one that I do not think was dangerous, but gave every appearance of being aggressive. It was always a relief to reach the fence at the east end of the lake.

It was a long tramp and weighed down with tackle, bivvy, cooking equipment, food and bait it was a joy to sink down at the water's edge.

Nearly always present, apart from the large flock of resident coots was a family of shelducks. It was strange that they chose to rear their ducklings so far from the coast. They are beautiful birds, larger than a mallard with bright scarlet bills, dark green heads, the rest patterned black and white apart from a warm orange band around the breast.

I was fascinated watching them, as with their rather nondescript fluffy young they patrolled the lake. The ducklings vociferously following their parents, a little flotilla of blotched light and dark grey balls bobbing on the ripples.

Surface or paddling ducks such as mallard, and shelducks are also of this persuasion, rarely dive except when in extreme danger. I discovered that their young were proficient divers where groundbait was concerned. Vic Bellars has since told me that when he was fishing the Marsh with maggots as bait a young duckling took his bait. While reeling in so that the youngster could be released one of the parents launched an intimidating low level attack. Unfortunately this shelduck flew into the line and became entangled. This was a pretty pickle indeed, one furious duck becoming more and more entwined as it tried to free itself, while its offspring, cheeping loudly, was flapping around on the surface. After a hectic minute or so, Vic having to suffer a series of painful pecks, the parent bird was untangled and put in Vic's haversack so that it could not come to further harm. The duckling was luckily only hooked in its bill, so without any damage to either bird they were released together.

Hungry ducks were not the only problem encountered when fishing the Marsh. Because the water was extremely shallow, these shallows extending for many yards from the bank, the tench tended to stay in the deeper water some sixty to eighty yards out.

This was tench fishing different from any I had done before. Float fishing at such a range was quite impracticable, besides fishing the dark hours could be productive too. The local anglers had found a method and this had already accounted for large tench of seven pounds and over being landed.

In the chapter on barbel I have described how I have caught them on swimfeeder tackle; the swimfeeder when packed full of maggots and plugged with just moistened breadcrumb gave sufficient weight to cast the long distances necessary to reach those areas where the tench fed at the Marsh.

In order to bait up a swim so far out into the lake the feeder was filled time and time again, cast out, and allowed to empty its contents until a carpet of bait covered a small area of the lake bed. Then a last cast was made with the feeder filled once more, so that the baited hook lay among the free offerings. The rods were set in two rod rests, tips pointing at the bait and in order to indicate if a tench picked up the baited hook an indicator bobbin was clipped to the line between two rod rings. The bobbin was then pulled down, so it hung some 12 to 18 inches below the rod. This bobbin was either anchored to the ground with a short length of line or the line secured to the base of one of the rod rests, so that when the rod was lifted from the rests to strike into a fish the bobbin dropped clear.

The indicator signalled a bite by rising, sometimes so fast that it smacked into the rod, but bites at the Marsh were never numerous and the bobbin hung motionless, often for hours at a time. Staring at unmoving bobbins for long periods is tiring, inevitably one's attention is distracted and so often as to seem uncanny, that is the very moment a tench decides to take the bait. Usually such bites are missed, the strike too late. To overcome having to keep one's eyes glued to the bobbin, the front rod rest head was of a type that incorporated an electronic indicator, 'buzzers' as anglers call them. This is no place to describe the technicalities of such a device, but buzzers bleep the moment the bait is touched and a tiny red light glows. Even if the angler is drowsy or enjoying watching the wildlife on the lake, that first bleep alerts him instantly, then he can transfer his gaze to the bobbin which will tell him whether he has a real bite or if it was just a fish brushing against the line. For night fishing an indicator bobbin containing a beta light was also used. This glowed pale green, and the darker the night the brighter it seemed to shine.

There was another drawback to long range fishing at the Marsh which I had never encountered before: floating weed. This built up in rafts clogging the line where it entered the water. Even sinking the rod tip below the surface did little to mitigate the problem, for this weed was thick and glutinous and much of it drifted along under the surface. The only way to cure the problem was to stake out a long keepnet upwind of the line, so the weed gathering against the mesh was arrested, leaving the line clear.

Jim Tyree with a big Norfolk lake tench taken on swimfeeder and sweetcorn.

Father and son, Dave and Neil Plummer with two big Norfolk tench
that fell to sweetcorn.

During this first visit I met Paul Belston, a young angler who was fishing the side of the lake opposite to me. We chatted about our prospects and the lake's potential as anglers will and I came to know Paul well. I persevered with fishing maggots and, using a swimfeeder, was casting well out into the middle of the lake. However, although I hooked a couple of fish, certainly good tench, I did not manage to land them, perhaps because I was using tackle that was too light to cope with those hefty Marsh fish.

Two weeks later I made the long drive from Rotherham to Norfolk once again. Prepared for a long stay I camped on the bankside. Sweetcorn had by now become known as a superb tench bait and I pre-baited heavily with the golden coloured grains. At first the tench did not appear to be interested in this new source of food, but now it was to become the best bait for the water. So it was fortuitous that I had chosen to try sweetcorn just at the time the tench decided they wanted sweetcorn and little else.

Martyn Page, a Norwich angler who was fishing close by persevered with sweetcorn in spite of the fact that in earlier years he had landed some fine tench using maggots. While I was chatting to him, he had a fast confident bite; sweetcorn it appeared was going to work.

After my earlier experience losing fish because my tackle was not man enough for the job, I had increased my line strength to 4-lb breaking strain. My small but very strong forged No 12 hook was knotted to a 3-lb hook length. That very morning I landed three superb tench, the largest was a magnificent fish that missed being my longed-for seven pounder by a whisker, just half an ounce. I now realized that if I was going to catch my 7-lb tench I must be prepared to travel to those waters where such fish existed, however far from home they might be. I was by now a dyed in the wool, dedicated angler with a driving ambition—to catch large fish whatever the species.

There are many ways of discovering where large fish are being caught. The angling press is of course a good source of information. Editors thrive on reports of outstanding catches and the anglers responsible, unless they are part of the big fish scene are not loathe to have their prowess publicised. However, some set out purposely to deceive, stating that they caught such and such a specimen from 'a water in Norfolk' when in fact it was taken in Surrey!

But still the most reliable source of information remained the grapevine.

So it was I came to hear of a gravel pit near Oxford called, uninspiringly, the T.C. pit. Here was a beautiful lake, its maturity belying its short existence, for it had been formed as a result of gravel extraction to provide aggregate for the extensive road system that encompassed the city. It seemed large after the Marsh and extended to some twenty acres; it was certainly deeper, but like the Marsh and so many good tench waters it was very weedy.

One of the more normal features in such pits are the parallel subsurface gravel bars resulting from the gravel extraction process. The trenches between the bars are channels which fish use as they move from one part of the water to another. When the top of a bar is shallow enough for weed beds to grow the base of such a bar is usually one of the best places to distribute groundbait. Weedy bars are certainly attractive to fish and in particular tench.

The T.C. pit was more famous for the large bream it contained, but there was a good stock of tench some reputed to reach the then magical 7-lb mark. Because this water was so far from home I could only fish when I had the time, such as during a holiday or if I considered the weather augured well, a weekend visit was always possible.

Any new water that is unfamiliar needs time to access; fish are not evenly distributed throughout the lake, so just a fleeting visit was unlikely to produce startling results. First the depths had to be checked then the variation of bottom features and the location of likely looking gravel bars and weed beds ascertained. When all this had been achieved, and it takes time, a decision could be made as to where to place the groundbait. I really needed longer, but I was only able to spend four days on my first visit to T.C. In order not to miss an hour of fishing time I camped by the lake, erecting the bivvy right at the water's edge. Using two rods I decided to try out a different tackle rig on each. Both incorporated a swimfeeder. The simple link ledger has already been mentioned and this was used for it had stood me in good stead in the past, and I felt confident using familiar tackle. On the second rod I experimented with different hook lengths allied to a paternoster rig. This rig has the weight, in this case a swimfeeder, at the extremity of the line. The hook length is secured to the line or may be free-running by passing through a swivel connected to the paternoster link. This link comprises the weight at one end, while the other end is knotted to the swivel. So paternosters can be fixed or running, according to one's fancy.

For groundbait I used maggots and casters mixed into balls of moistened breadcrumbs. As an added attraction breadcrumbs can be flavoured with essences; these can be sweet, fruit, meat or fish based. Casters are the pupae of the bluebottle fly, maggots are the larvae.

71

Three tench between 7lb and 7lb 8-oz from Johnson's Lake Kent, that fell to boilies.

A pupae is the inactive stage of development between larva and insect, as a chrysalis is the stage between caterpillar and butterfly. Castors can also be used as a hook bait for many species and tench are no exception. But on this first visit to T.C. I played safe and used maggots on the hook, a bait that I had caught so many tench on in the past. Both front rod rests had optonic heads, the latest sensitive buzzers, that bleeped their warning if a fish even gently tweaked the bait. But if a fish took the bait confidently and swam off giving a 'run' as anglers say, the bleeps merged into a continuous high-pitched urgent note. Indicator bobbins, their 18 retaining lines fixed to the rear rod rests were positioned to hand some eighteen inches below the rods which were set in the rests with their tips pointing at the baits.

Unlike the Marsh long distance casting was unnecessary as the fish-attracting gravel bars were in many cases close to the bankside. I was happy with the swim I had selected, which was situated no more than twenty-five yards away.

On that first day all my preparations, the expense and the tedious journey from Yorkshire were amply repaid. Tench were caught in plenty, some of the size I was accustomed to from northern waters but even small tench fight tenaciously. Best of all I landed a beautiful, muscular specimen that pulled the needle of the dial weighing scales down to register 6 lb 5 oz.

During the following three days I enjoyed many hours sitting beside that tranquil lake, every now and again the buzzers bleeped, the bobbins sailed upwards and as I bent the rod into yet another tench I fervently hoped it would be larger than I had caught before. It was not to be, and on subsequent visits I had to spend many a day before my first seven pounder from T.C. lay dark green and gleaming in the folds of my landing net.

Of the huge bream, I saw little and not one deigned to sample my baits, but a fine striped perch, dorsal fin erect in indignation did; it weighed a most respectable $1^1/_2$ lb.

The T.C. pit was yet another milestone along the route to a huge tench and I learnt much from fishing there. I was always full of anticipation when fishing this water and apart from the six and seven pounders the average size of the tench I caught was far better than I was accustomed to. The T.C. tench were catholic in their tastes, apart from maggots they were happy to take worms, even large fat lobworms or even flake. Flake is the crumb of a fresh loaf of white bread. It swells when immersed in water making a highly visible bait. A piece of bread without crust will float being naturally buoyant but if it is pressed between finger and thumb it will sink

slowly. When using flake as bait the centre of a piece of bread, in area near to the size of a 2p coin, is pressed in the middle. The hook is passed through this flattened part and for added security sometimes a little is pressed onto the shank of the hook. It has its advantages when fishing over bottom weed where a heavier bait would sink deep among the fronds to become invisible. Flake sinks slowly coming to rest lightly on top of the weeds where fish can see it easily. Baits festooned with weed are unattractive and fish tend to ignore them.

I had by now moved to Norfolk, so I was at least a little nearer to T.C. However, through rumours and final confirmation via the grapevine I learnt that a lake in Kent was beginning to produce some very large tench indeed. This was yet another gravel pit, some eight acres in extent. This water could be fished on a season or day ticket basis and was a well-known carp fishery, named Johnson's after the man who owned it.

Like T.C. it was a typical gravel pit with subsurface bars quite deep averaging seven to eight feet, with even deeper holes. Johnson's, which I first fished in the early 80s, was surrounded by bankside shrubs while the margins were either sandy or consisted of fine gravel. It was a heavily weeded water, the main species being Canadian pondweed, which is dense, fast growing and a particularly good oxygenator. Because this weed can cover much of the bottom of any lake where it is established it can cause problems for anglers using bottom baits. As you will see this little hazard can be circumvented. But before I explain just how we managed this, a word about this popular fishery. Because it contained some fine carp it was pre-baited very heavily by those anglers seeking some of the large fish that were present. Literally thousands of high protein, high-nutrition value baits and boilies, some of exotic flavours were introduced by the carp men. The tench in Johnson's, and there was a good stock of them, found these baits to their liking. In fact so much so they began to take little interest in natural food, but became preoccupied with this abundance of nutritional largesse. Furthermore, it was showered into the lake when the tench fed most freely, in the warmer months.

Anglers could make up their own baits, but because so many waters had been stocked with carp and the numbers of anglers fishing for carp had increased dramatically, boilie baits were being made commercially. Now baits could be obtained from fishing tackle retailers. The boilie boom had arrived. Normally carp baits were marble sized up to 18 mm in diameter, but it was not long before mini boilies became available.

These baits, a little larger than a fat garden pea, suited the tench perhaps even more than the larger baits. The carp anglers soon found that they were catching more tench than carp but it was of course of their own doing. It was not long before the tench in Johnson's lake began to increase in size and weight until it became known as one of the premier large tench waters in the country. With such a wealth of easily acquired food, those tench grew and grew until one lucky angler landed one of the undreamed-of weight of 9 lb 7 oz.

With the possibility of other tench reaching such a mammoth weight I decided that fish Johnson's I must, and soon I was camping beside the water whenever I could snatch a few days off work.

On my first trip I teamed up with Paul Belston who I had first encountered at the Marsh. We arrived after the 120-mile drive at mid-day one Sunday. I had grown used to travelling long distances but with even the remote possibility of catching just one enormous tench I could have happily driven three times as far. We spent the first two hours walking around the margins of the lake. We found two well-known Norfolk anglers, Chris Turnbull who is no mean artist when it comes to painting fish, and has illustrated angling books, and Jim Bigden, both fishing from a point of land that protruded from the shore. From this vantage point both deep sand shallows could be cast to.

It proved to be one of the best swims on the lake. Chris and Jim were due to leave for home shortly, having spent a whole week at the water. This was good news for Paul and me, for not only could we move into what appeared to be an excellent swim but it had been liberally laced with regular supplies of free offerings in the form of the boilies of which the tench had become so fond.

We had brought along our home-made boilie baits, which were made semi-buoyant by adding eggs to the mix before the quick plunge into boiling water for a minute or so. Buoyant baits can be anchored so they rise just above the bottom weed and such baits were to prove their worth in this respect, combating the all-enveloping Canadian pondweed.

For fishing on the clear areas among the weeds the baits could be made neutrally buoyant; they rested gently on the bottom but any current caused by the waving tail of a feeding fish, or even the displacement of water by a fish passing over or by them caused them to rise a little and waft around. The tench could never resist such baits.

To come to terms with the big tench in Johnson's we used what was in effect a carp fishing technique. The boilie was not put on the hook at all but was connected to it by what is known as a 'hair'. The hair consists of a length of very fine 1.1 lb breaking strain monofilament or dacron line. There is a small loop at one end of this hair which is pushed through the bait with a boilie needle. A small stub of thicker line, silicone tube or even in an emergency a piece of grass is placed in the loop which is pulled back till the stub rests against the bait. This 'stop' as it is called prevents the bait flying off the hair when casting. The hair can now be tied to the hook either to the hook bend itself or to the hook eye. Usually the length of the hair can vary from one to two inches. We fished our baits on a hair of one and a half inches.

The idea of fishing baits on a hair was to overcome the problems encountered by anglers fishing hard-fished waters where the carp would not take the bait with a hook in it. They would pick up loose baits freely enough, leaving any bait with a hook in it untouched. Various theories were debated in carp angling circles as to how the carp could differentiate between baits with hooks in them and those without. Some said the fish could tell the difference in weight, others that after being in water for some time, the water reacted with the steel hook and tainted the bait. Whatever the reason, the solution to the problem was solved, and those using the hair found that catching wary carp was easier than before. The reason the baits fished on the hair rig were successful was due to the manner in which a carp takes a bait. Normally a carp approaches the bait then stops some inches away, and if it decides to eat it will suck hard taking in a quantity of water which is expelled via the gills. This sharp intake of water lifts the bait which is swept into the carp's mouth. The hook follows and is nicely positioned just inside the mouth as the carp passes the bait backward prior to swallowing. But a carp which can suck in a bait quickly, is equally capable of ejecting it if it is suspicious, spitting out the bait so fast that an angler cannot possibly set the hook, however fast his reaction.

Carp anglers began to experience tentative bites even when using the hair. This problem too was overcome and in a most ingenious way. There has been much discussion on the ethics of what was termed the 'bolt rig'. This rig caused suspicious carp to hook themselves as they moved off having taken a bait. Very simply the line was passed through the swivelling eye of a much heavier weight than would normally be used, usually $1^1/2$-2 ounces. A carp could pull the line through the eye but only so far, for the angler placed a backstop some 12-18 inches behind the weight. When a carp swam off with the bait it was suddenly checked as the back stop reached the heavy lead. This resistance caused the hook to begin to penetrate; feeling this, the carp bolted towing the weight and driving in the hook so that it obtained a secure hold.

Bites on the bolt rig are invariably fast and the anti-reverse mechanism on the reel must be in the 'off' position so that the handle can revolve backwards. This allows line to be taken from the spool.

Bolt rig bites are very impressive; the bobbin flies up and the reel handle whirrs round. The carp men call such bites 'churners'. When the rod is lifted from the rests the carp is almost always hooked, so there is no need to strike.

While hair rigs and bolt rigs are successful methods for catching carp they are equally as effective for other fish, including tench.

In order to catch Johnson's tench both Paul and I used hairs in conjunction with a bolt rig. We also found that baits with a sweet flavour such as mini boilies with the exotic name of fruit cocktail or vanilla flavoured baits were popular with the tench. We fished for three days and both of us caught three fine tench, seven pounders—the largest of 7 lb 7 oz was an outstanding fish at that time.

Johnson's was a popular fishery with easy access to the many keen carp and tench anglers living comparatively close to London. The reports of such large fish being caught with some regularity encouraged more and more anglers to fish the water. We soon learnt to avoid the competition for the best fishing positions as well as the crowd of anglers by avoiding fishing at weekends. For the next few years we travelled to Johnson's for midweek sessions lasting three or four days, trying new areas and new methods in the hope of landing even bigger fish. Sometimes the big tench showed themselves by rolling at the surface and baits cast out to where they patrolled were always likely to be taken. Tench do keep to well-defined patrol routes, particularly in gravel pits. As our familiarity with the lake grew we could lay an ambush by baiting up and fishing where the tench were known to pass.

Keen as we were to fish, whenever we arrived at the lake our first task was to gather up the litter discarded by irresponsible anglers. Why is it that we have become a nation of litterbugs? Indeed the problem has become so widespread that fisheries have had to be closed as the piles of rubbish mounted. I think that in the main anglers are better than most, but there are still a minority of uncaring fishermen, deaf to all appeals, who make the non-angling public think that all of us are tarred with the same brush. Johnson's was a beautiful place, and we did all we could to keep it so.

Perhaps what pleased us most was that we could still catch large tench in the traditional ways. Often we could dispense with the ultra-efficient baits and terminal tackle and sit quietly, float fishing the margins with the old well-tried simple baits as of yore.

I had by now become slotted into a groove believing that to capture large fish it was usually necessary to travel far from home. Here I was living in a country with a wealth of fine waters yet travelling hundreds of miles a year just to go fishing. But then the grass is always greener as the old adage affirms, and I was blinkered to the fine fishing on my doorstep. Steve Brown who lives in Norwich decided to see if an excellent carp lake, one of a chain of waters along the Wensum valley on the outskirts of the city, contained big tench. Certainly it had some tench swimming its waters, it remained to be seen if there were larger fish present.

The carp anglers had, as carp anglers will, been piling in the boilies. It seemed that the most obvious tactic was to pre-bait with the more tench-sized mini boilies, as the fish must have become accustomed to consuming many of the baits destined for the carp.

The season opened on June 16th, and some weeks in advance Steve and I carried out a pretty thorough survey, noted likely-looking swims and carried out a little judicious bankside clearance of the overgrown margins. As June approached our pre-baiting campaign commenced; occasionally twice, sometimes three times a week we catapulted the mini boilies into those areas, mainly gravel bars, where we had seen a few tench roll at the surface. On each visit two to three hundred baits were introduced, we hoped they would draw tench into the swims and that they would become preoccupied with these flavoured baits by the time the season opened.

This gravel pit, known locally as Taverham No 3, was of medium size, it seemed, surrounded by a woodland of mature oak, beech, ash and particularly fine birch trees, a timeless secluded oasis. The banks were pleasant to fish from, dry and sandy. Tree-girt, lily-studded inlets led from the main body of the lake where huge carp heaved clear of the water and fell back, with a shattering crash, the displaced water erupting into ever widening, wavelike ripples.

Because we wanted to make sure that we could fish over our pre-baited swims Steve arrived at the waterside the day before the season opened. He had many hours of waiting before I arrived at mid-morning with plenty of time on my hands to set up my tackle prior to my first cast of the season, at midnight. We only put out a few baits, otherwise the tench might never have found our hookbaits with so many others to choose from; it would have been looking for the proverbial needle.

It was a still warm night, overcast, so not a star reflected in the calm surface. I cast one bait some sixty yards out so that it rested at the base of one of the pre-baited bars, then the other to a bar much nearer, just thirty-five yards away.

The optonics were set, indicators adjusted. Tingling and tense I awaited developments. Disappointingly, only one small tench fell for the mini boilies. Then as the sky imperceptibly lightened to disclose a mist-laden dawn, the bait on the faraway bar was taken. The buzzer's high-pitched bleeps merged into one continuous tone which ceased abruptly as I grabbed the rod from the rests and swept it back over my shoulder. The hook took hold and a large fish, certainly no tench, began to take line from the reel with powerful surging runs. It was a hard fight before a large-scaled bronze-flanked carp of 23 lb graced my net. Re-casting I caught one more little tench, then fish activity appeared to cease and the lake lay before us, deathly still. Steve had not even had a bite.

We fished on through the day, dozing occasionally, then out of the blue the buzzer which had been so quiescent bleeped again. This time, hoping against hope for a large tench I had to be content with yet another carp, a fine fully scaled mirror carp that weighed just over 10 lb.

So we stayed fishing hard. The following day we noted bigger tench rolling which encouraged us mightily, big tench were in the lake after all. The weather became fine and hot, and there was much bankside disturbance from other anglers. Because Steve's swim had proved so unproductive he came and joined me. After an uneventful night followed by a glorious dawn, the tench arrived at the bars. I landed my largest Norfolk tench, so near to 8 lb, that registered 7 lb 14^1/$_2$ oz on the dial scales. I then caught another lovely fish of 6 lb 8 oz and other slightly smaller. Steve's luck had changed, he landed tench, the best scaled over 6 lb.

I continued to fish throughout the rest of the summer whenever I could find the odd few hours, often in the early morning before work. I baited and fished other parts of the lake, and while fishing in a swim adjacent to the bar swims, where Steve and I had started the season I caught my largest tench.

July had all but passed, I had caught fish in plenty but none larger than my near eight pound fish. Then, when I was beginning to wonder if there were any even larger fish in the lake, my dream of catching an 8-lb tench was fulfilled. She was thickset, muscular with a tail like a wallpaper pasting brush and when the tussle was over and she grudgingly gave up the struggle, I netted the largest tench I have ever caught: 8 lb 2 oz.

Taverham seemed a well balanced fishery containing large fish of many other species. One day a 2-lb roach decided to sample the mini boilie on my hook, this was an unexpected bonus. A large bream did likewise, this latter fish weighed an impressive 11 lb 6 oz. By September, with nights becoming cooler my thoughts began to turn to the great pike of the Broads, and perhaps a little reluctantly I left this beautiful lake, my ambition to catch an 8-lb tench had been fulfilled and I was content.

Early in 1987, Clive Diedrich a nationally known carp angler and proprietor of the Richworth Bait Company contacted me. He offered me the chance to make a film on catching tench; this seemed to me a challenge, which would if all went well be a most exciting venture.

Clive controlled a 25-acre lake, holding a prolific stock of tench. Called Shroaders this water was like Taverham, a Wensum valley lake. The surroundings were similar too, for Shroaders was a gravel pit with heavily wooded banks and certainly the rafts of water lilies were even more extensive. Any angler seeing Shroaders for the first time would imagine it was a perfect lake for carp and tench and so it was. It was also an excellent choice for film making, being so heavily stocked with fish. A fishing film needs to show fish being caught, not shots of an angler waiting hour after hour even if the eventual result is a large fish on the bank. To be successful a fishing film must be full of action, with several fish being hooked, played and landed.

Heading the team of film makers was Jonathan Harris ex-BBC cameraman, who also acted as director. He brought along an assistant, a keen enthusiastic young man who dealt with lens changes and similar activities. Stan, a retired BBC sound engineer handled that side of the operation and Annie was responsible for the script and continuity. I invited my business partner, Derrick Amies to act as a man friday, helping me with tackle and acting as boatman.

Eventually, it was decided to start a whole week's filming commencing on the first Sunday in July. Well before the team assembled I selected suitable swims and cleared some of the bottom weed by raking it ashore. I used a metal, T-shaped, home-made rake with a spread of three feet. It was heavy, even heavier to pull ashore when festooned with half a hundredweight of weed and mud. The rake which was secured to a length of rope was heaved out into the lake then hauled ashore. I could just manage to throw it about twenty yards.

Shroader's tench were renowned for their appreciation of sweetcorn, but as I wanted to demonstrate the use of mini boilies for tench fishing I pre-baited my chosen swims with those the week before the filming was due to commence. As the tench were used to feeding on bright yellow grains I selected a mini boilie of the same colour with the exotic name of Honey Yucatan. I have to admit I distributed these little yellow baits with some trepidation, wondering if the tench would decide that they were good to eat.

On the Sunday evening we all met at the Swan in Horning, primarily so that we could meet for the first time in a pleasant social atmosphere and of course discuss the script. It was immediately obvious that the team would work in harmony, and my natural apprehensions at having to catch fish to order and in front of a critical audience was at least partially allayed. Slightly keyed up I arrived at the lake at 6 a.m. I was certainly taken aback by the sight of a large mobile crane complete with caged platform which could be elevated to some 50 feet above the ground. However this monster, Jon's idea, was to prove its worth that day in spite of being temperamental. It took its time when the platform needed to be lowered.

That first day Jon filmed from the crane—from such a vantage point he could pan every nook and cranny. Then as a finale he zoomed in on me as I approached the first swim and began to speak.

It all seemed so simple, but Jon is a perfectionist and he was rarely satisfied. Takes were ruined by the noise of a car passing along the lane and on that particular day the aircraft from RAF Coltishall decided that the sky over Shroaders was a fine place to perform.

At 1 p.m. we paused for lunch, it seemed after many hours Jon was still not satisfied and I began to get some inkling of the time and effort needed to film even a short sequence. Eventually all was well and I spent the rest of the day being filmed as I walked the lake margins, describing the swims and my reasons for choosing them. This was followed by my doing a little pre-baiting. By now 13 or 14 hours had passed by; this filming lark was far harder than I ever imagined, I felt very weary. I decided that for the legering sequence—legered baits lie on the bottom—I would fish with two rods, each with a different tackle rig. On one baits would be on the hair, allied to a bolt rig, carp style. On the other rod I used the more conventional paternoster, the more normal weight at the extremity of the line being replaced by a swimfeeder.

By first light on the Tuesday with rod rests positioned and only a very few baits scattered into the swim I was ready to perform but still secretly worried that the tench would ignore my baits. With the short baiting up sequence 'in the can' the filming began with me casting, then adjusting the optonic and setting the bobbin indicator so that it hung down some 15 to 18 inches beneath the rod. I eased myself down into my fishing chair ready to bait up, and bring my other rod into play. There just wasn't time, the optonic bleeped, the bobbin rose smartly and I was on my feet with bent rod in my hands. By now, the camera forgotten, I was playing a tench, it was as if I was quite alone. That tench was a plump well conditioned female, she weighed 4 lb exactly. All my earlier fear dissipated, I began to enjoy myself. I could hardly believe I had been so fortunate, nothing to this catching fish to order I thought, as with the next four casts I landed four tench of similar size. There was no doubt that the Honey Yucatan baits were proving amazingly successful. As for the tench it seemed they all wanted to become extras, or perhaps a better description might be stars, they just queued up to get on camera!

So I fished on, generally finding it impossible to use two rods as the moment I cast out a bait on one, that bait was eagerly taken. With occasional breaks for camera repositioning, and describing tackle rigs, which were placed on a large card balanced on my knees, two hours passed swiftly. It all appeared so easy and I was at pains to explain how rarely such events occur.

There was little rest for me for reporter, Adrian Curtiss, with cameraman in tow arrived. They wanted a feature for their paper on making fishing films. Adrian, a cheerful character who is full of banter and not averse to mickey-taking, wisecracked away as quite incredibly I caught seven or eight tench. 'You order them, I'll catch them' I thought. I wondered how long I would have to keep up this tench catching game but Adrian with a full spool of exposed film in the can, was more than content and I settled back in my chair to relax.

Film makers never seem satisfied, so all the afternoon I was casting, placing rods in rests, adjusting the optonics and bobbins. Then followed sequences of handling and weighing fish, and how to return them to the water unharmed.

By the evening I felt that I had never worked so hard for so long in all my life.

The next day was to be devoted to float fishing. I had already selected a deep, 7 to 8-foot swim beside a small island so the boat was required and Derrick became an indispensable member of the team. Jon's plan was to film me with the camera placed beside me, then later he would try to get more sequences by shooting from the boat.

Tackle was changed to a 13-foot match rod, set up to fish the lift method. The by now proven Honey Yucatan boilies were joined to the hook by a hair yet again. The line was fine, only 3 lb breaking strain and I wanted to demonstrate how to use the old fashioned centre pin reel, a joy to use and so different from the modern-day fixed-spool types.

Of course it was the crack of day again when we were ready to start, by now entirely confident I was not at all surprised to find the island swim frothing with bubbles from feeding tench; fate was smiling on us.

Somehow quite sure I should catch one of those bubbling tench, I cast, placed the rod in the rests, and turned the reel handle so that the float cocked vertically with about an inch of its brightly coloured tip showing proud of the surface. It must have been perfect for Jon as he filmed the motionless float with bubbles erupting around it. For while the camera was running the float started to rise, then overbalanced and fell flat on the surface. It was a classic bite, and the ensuing fight resulting in the capture of a 4 lb 8 oz tench was filmed from the cast to the landing of the fish without interruption. The film crew were delighted.

I was worried that when the boat was used it would scare the fish. But Derrick exploited his boat handling skills to the full. I'm sure only his expertise enabled the filming to be so effective. He manoeuvred the boat with infinite care and hardly a ripple to within a few yards of my float while the tench continued to feed.

Clive Diedrich arrived with his partner Bob so we adjourned to a pub for a chat about events to date and our plans for the next day. All went swimmingly and at last Derrick and I plus the whole team, together with my wife Linda celebrated on the evening of our last day.

It had been both a worrying and an exhilarating experience for me, naturally not having been involved in any form of dramatic entertainment, let alone been the lead player, I was at first extremely apprehensive. I came to understand the patience, skill and sheer dedication, not to mention the vast amount of time required to make a film. I became the greatest of friends with the whole team and they earned my grateful thanks for their tact and understanding, even if at times they were hard taskmasters. Perhaps I should also thank the tench for performing so well!

That week was one of the most interesting and exciting fishing trips I've ever encountered. I can still hardly believe how successful it proved to be. However, I shall have to face the camera yet again; already Clive and the team are planning a pike fishing film to be shot at Loch Lomond. I'm full of confidence now, but I'm pretty sure I shall suffer from just a little stage fright when we go afloat on that beautiful loch some day in 1988.

Barbel: Strong, Hard-Fighting Fish of Fast Flowing Rivers

In 1655 the Speaker of the House of Commons said: 'Cosmographers do agree that this island is incomparably furnished with pleasant rivers, like veins in the National body, which convey the blood into all parts, whereby the whole is nourished and made useful.'

England may not boast of mighty rivers such as the Mississippi, Nile, Rhine or Danube, but though insignificant streams in comparison, ours do have a wealth of individual character and diversity denied those great water courses.

From mountain, hill and fell our rivers rush ever downward, foam flecked and bubbling, chattering over their stony beds, cascading over rock ledges then plunging as waterfalls into deep mysterious pools, the home of speckled trout. Yet so varied are the contours of our land that not far away another river glides serenely by tree-lined banks, meanders through lush buttercup-dappled water meadows and long green fronds of streamer weed wave languorously in the gentle current. In summer, swallows kiss the surface and the watermint and meadowsweet scent the air.

As the Speaker said so long ago, rivers are the lifeblood of the nation: they have watered our land, powered the ancient corn mills and served as highways to transport heavy loads. Without a river, Stonehenge could not have been built.

Rivers are a heritage we must protect, but alas, succeeding generations have paid scant attention to the words of that sage parliamentarian. Since the Industrial Revolution we have turned so many of our rivers into open sewers carrying human and industrial effluent, that even the vastness of the oceans are affected. We have destroyed the salmon runs; in all our larger rivers this kingly fish once swam. In the Middle Ages did not the London apprentices complain that they were given Thames salmon far too often?

Perhaps it is not too late, conservation is a growing and popular cause.

Nature, ever resilient, needs but little help to repair the damage done by the one life form on this planet which seems hell bent on destroying its own environment.

What is a *Barbus Barbus?* Ask that question of anyone and 99 per cent of them would not have the faintest idea. You could well get answers as varied as, 'a character from the Arabian Nights', or, 'I think it must be a kind of prickly cactus'. *Barbus Barbus* is the scientific name for the barbel—an apt description because the four tentacle-like protuberances hanging from each side of its mouth are called barbules. These organs are sensitive and efficient receptors enabling the fish to locate its food on the river bed.

The barbel is indigenous to the European rivers from the Rhine to the Danube and the Russian rivers flowing into the Azov and Black Seas. The barbel can tolerate high temperatures and can be found as far south as Spain. Before our island became separated from the continent, the Trent and the Thames were tributaries of the Rhine, part of the long extinct great North Sea river.

So the barbel is native to England but only in those rivers flowing east that were part of a much larger European river system. The Yorkshire rivers and the Trent, the Thames and its tributaries were once the only barbel rivers in the kingdom. But the species is now more widely spread due to their introduction by Water Authorities to other rivers such as the Hampshire Stour and Avon, the westward-flowing Severn and latest of all Norfolk's Wensum.

The barbel, while it can exist in still water thrives best in running water. Its long streamlined shape, flattened head and triangular body in cross-section, have evolved to enable the species to live in fast water. The barbel rides the current, holdings its position by using the minimum amount of energy.

Barbel can grow large, a fish weighing 10 lb is considered a specimen, but larger fish have been seen and once, in the close season for coarse fish, a salmon angler hooked and landed a magnificent fish of 17 lb.

Barbel are powerful fish—when hooked they will fight to exhaustion and the barbel angler will try to land his fish before it becomes totally drained of energy. Even so, it's often necessary to hold a barbel, head facing the current, until it regains enough strength to swim away.

I caught my first barbel in Yorkshire. The county is well-endowed with rivers holding the species and the Yorkshire rivers are unique in their similarities. Because of the rain clouds that sweep in on the prevailing south-westerly winds and empty their contents over the hills, these northern rivers can change from a gentle stream to a raging torrent in hours. Rivers can rise many feet in a day and like the highland rivers of Scotland, those in Yorkshire are subject to heavy and unexpected spates. But when the waters subside and the suspended sediment begins to clear, the fishing is at its best.

I was very young, just 14 years old, when I first went barbel fishing. The local angling club used to run a coach at weekends. Leaving Rotherham, it used to do a round tour dropping off fishermen at various places on the rivers Ouse and Nidd. While the Nidd did not hold barbel as large as could be found elsewhere, it contained many small to medium-sized fish. For a keen youngster, it was a fine river on which to serve a barbel-fishing apprecticeship.

I still remember vividly my first sight of the Nidd. It was set in unspoilt countryside and the bleating of sheep, the sigh of the breeze in the bankside trees and the ceaseless murmur of running water was so unlike the bustle and grime of industrial Rotherham that I was spellbound. The river rippled over the shallows, slipped quietly by in the deeper pools with cream-coloured bubble clusters, like froth on a glass of Guinness, sliding ever seaward.

I found a glide of slower running, deeper water on a bend in the river. Settling down on the bank a few yards upstream, I threw a few handfuls of creamy white, wriggling maggots into the river, so that as they sank, they twisted and turned, eventually reaching the bottom to trickle along in the current. I then put two maggots on a tiny hook, sharp as a needle, and setting my red-topped float so that the bait would just trip the bottom, I allowed the float to ride the current, paying out line as it began its voyage downstream. This method of fishing is called trotting. Often the line has to be lifted from the surface by raising the rod—'mending the line' in anglers' parlance. The bait should follow the line of the free offerings that are already being taken eagerly by fish attracted to easily acquired food.

My float reached the deeper glide, dipped once and disappeared. As I quickly lifted the rod, the line lightened and cut the surface leaving a V-shaped wake of tiny wavelets. I felt the electric tugs and thumps of an unseen fish that bent the rod into a hoop. That little barbel fought as all barbel do, long and hard, and because I was using such gossamer tackle it was many minutes before I was gazing at my first ever barbel. Its flanks were shot with golden scales, its large pale orange fins were erect in indignation, it was a jewel of a fish.

I was lucky that day, I landed nine barbel. The largest did not quite weigh 3 lb, and I had lost others purely because my light gear was inadequate.

From that day forward I dreamed barbel and for the next few years all of my spare time was devoted to fishing for them, not only in the Nidd, but in other Yorkshire rivers. I was keen and quite single-minded, I was prepared to fish and fish until that ambition was achieved. Needless to say it was many years before I succeeded.

No one river is exactly like another; each has its own characteristics and an angling technique that is excellent for one may not succeed to anything like the same extent in another. I tried new methods, read angling books, as well as features on barbel fishing in the weekly and monthly angling press, but above all I spent hours getting to know intimately, stretches of Yorkshire rivers reputed to hold larger-than-average fish. The public thinks angling is a matter of luck, but luck plays little part. It has been truly said that only 10 per cent of anglers catch 90 per cent of the larger fish. Those 10 per cent pay scant attention to chance. They catch their fish by single-minded dedication and effort. They know every depth, every quirk of the current, where the fish lie according to the water conditions and above all, they spend time at the waterside, often just looking— learning as well as actually fishing.

So over the years I could soon identify a stretch of water and assess accurately its barbel potential, without so much as casting a bait into the river. At weekends I used to attend fishing matches, noting at the end-of-contest weigh-in those swims that had produced barbel. Often these areas were well worth fishing and I also came by such means to discover barbel-holding areas in the larger more featureless rivers such as the Yorkshire Ouse. It was quite noticeable that, although this river did not appear to alter in character for mile after mile, only selected stretches held the bigger fish.

One part of the Ouse I enjoyed fishing was at Newton. Newton is a typical Yorkshire village of grey stone dwellings, the fields bordering the river are enclosed by moss-covered stone walls, skilfully built without mortar, blending with the remote vales as if they were natural rocky outcrops. Ancient gnarled and twisted hawthorn trees shaded the livestock and at the beginning of the fishing season in June the trees were pendulous with sweet-scented blossom.

The river at Newton, set in a dale valley, was quieter and more mature than the bubbling, hurrying Nidd. The Ouse was more sedate, meandering through wooded countryside, but quickening as it foamed over the weir at Linton. I found that the tree-lined stretch of river at Benningborough Park, downstream of Newton, to be a prolific barbel area and I concentrated on this part of the river, getting to know the nature of the bottom contours, the slacks and eddies and where the better barbel could be found.

I was now seventeen, and became friends with another young Yorkshire angler, Rob Welton. Rob was a keen member of a specimen group who lived in Clifton, a small village near York. As I lived far away from the Ouse and even this wider, more slowly flowing river was subject to heavy flooding, I often made a phone call to Rob in order to obtain up-to-date information on the state of the river, and so save a wasted journey. Then too, Rob would call me when conditions were near perfect for barbel fishing.

We both became friendly with the landlord of an inn near the river. He was an angler at heart, loved to fish when his duties allowed and we talked fish and fishing as anglers will. He knew the river well, and his advice on barbel locations saved much of our valuable time. I usually called in at tea time before an evening's fishing so that I left for the riverbank relaxed and all the keener for mine host's encouragement.

Not only did I fish the evening hours, watching the oncoming dusk soften and blur the vale, but remained fishing on into the night. Because of the great trees overhanging the water, the darkness felt solid, stygian, and with every sound magnified it could be an eerie, even frightening experience at times. The sudden splash of a rising fish could shatter the silence and even the rustling of some small rodent in the undergrowth could sound like a large wild animal on the prowl. One fished with an easier mind with a companion.

All the time I fished I was learning to read the river by noting the strength of flow, the little turbulent eddies and the slow, dark, mysterious deeper pools. I could visualise the nature of the river bed with accuracy. Soon I got to know the crease in the current, that subtle surface change of pace where the water moved a shade slower than in mid-river, a favoured lie for barbel who could rest quietly but easily intercept morsels by moving out into the faster water, then slide back to more gentle holts.

Rob and I roamed the dales, and walked for mile after mile along the riverbank, but perhaps we spent more time fishing the Swale than any other river.

88

Early season barbel swim on the River Wensum above Norwich.

The Swale was a larger, wider edition of the Nidd. It was, as so many a northern river, subject to sudden spates. Debris such as tree branches were swept along in these floods until they became jammed, some caught up in living trees as the waters fell, while others, waterlogged, sank to the river bed to give cover and shelter from the current for the fish shoals. Many of the best barbel swims were full of tackle-snatching snags, and as spate succeeded spate these obstacles gathered further debris for our hooks to become tangled in.

A considerate farmer gave us permission to fish his water which turned and twisted through the fields where sheep and cattle fattened on the succulent grasses manured by the rich silt deposited by winter floods. The river banks were high and had been deeply undercut by the powerful current in times of flood. Apart from the snags, the bottom of the river was stony, some parts being of gravel or gravelly sand and as in all rivers in summer, full of waving waterweed.

Barbel love weeds, they shelter beneath the long streamers, moving onto the crystal clear gravelly runs between the beds to browse on the bottom algae, and wait for titbits to be borne to them by the current. Avoiding the heavily weeded stretches can be difficult and accurate casting to place a bait on the clear patches is a necessity. But such areas often harbour the largest fish. To catch them needs both stealth and pinpoint accuracy when casting. Weeds release oxygen during the daylight hours, provide shelter for the barbel from the direct rays of the sun and are an insectivore's larder, so we fished the little narrow runs between the weedbeds.

While the Swale barbel were not so plentiful as those in Yorkshire, their average size was greater. I now began to discover just how powerfully a 5-lb fish can fight and how it knows instinctively the shortest route to the thickest tangle of weeds or tree roots. We increased the strength of our lines and used larger, strongly forged hooks, but even so, we had to give some of those Swale fish best in the end. After grassing a 7-lb barbel during my first season fishing this fascinating river, I began to gain confidence and felt at last that I was becoming a barbel angler after all.

However, the really large fish reputed to inhabit the Swale's higher reaches never showed. We caught sizeable chub that fancied the baits intended for barbel and one memorable day I landed fourteen good-sized barbel, the largest not quite holding the needle of the weighing scales down to the 6-lb mark. But it was fun and everytime I fished, I added to my store of knowledge. I still trotted maggots downstream watching the scarlet float riding the current, but now I often fished with a bait lying still on the

bottom or if the weed allowed, let the current slowly roll the bait in an arc across the river bed. Always one method suited the day, the conditions and the mood of the fish; it paid to be versatile.

While maggots always caught the smaller fish we tried more substantial fare in the hope of attracting bigger fish. 'A big bait for a big fish' is an old angling adage, so we ledgered cubes of luncheon meat and balls of raw beef sausage meat stiffened with breadcrumbs, or sometimes sausage rusk or cheese paste. Naturally many free offerings were introduced and the barbel, not to mention the chub, soon discovered these meaty balls were tasty.

Our ledgering techniques improved and gradually we used float-fished maggots less and less. The tackle was as simple as we could devise. The line was passed through one eye of a small swivel, through a small bead then through the barrel of a ledger stop, a short length of plastic tube, and then the line was knotted to the hook. The ledger-stop barrel was plugged to hold it in place on the line some six inches from the hook. Four inches of line were attached to the bottom swivel eye to take the weights—large split shot which could be nipped on, so gripping the line. It was critical that only just enough shot was used to anchor the bait and hold still in the current. When a fish took the bait, the shot would move downstream helped by the flow of water, so little resistance would be encountered. For bites we watched our rod tips which would nod first as a barbel took the bait, then pull round sharply as the fish turned away downstream. Later we used more sensitive flexible rod tips; these quiver tips would register the most tentative of bites.

We now found fishing during the hours of darkness more productive. We could always fish our chosen swims for all other anglers had long departed. Because many fishermen do not 'study to be quiet' as Isaac Walton so wisely advised, they create much bankside disturbance and the barbel feed best in the dark hours. After the last footfalls had died away and day gave way to night, the barbel left the protective shelter of the streamer weed and roamed the river intent on feeding. So as to see our rod tips we taped a tiny radio-active isotope to them which glowed pale green, and by watching this and holding the line above the reel between finger and thumb we could not only see a bite but feel the gentle pluck as well. But staring at the little point of light was mesmerising, it appeared to nod and waver when it was in fact perfectly still. At first we struck at non-existent bites but soon learnt not to look directly at the beta lights, as they are called, but a little to one side. Barbel bites vary between

The current record Wensum barbel of 13 lb 6 oz in 1987.

An 11lb 7-oz Wensum barbel which fell to hair-rigged hemp and
sweetcorn.

full-blooded pulls on the rod bending it round, to a grating sensation, a trembling vibration perhaps interspersed with delicate twitches. These would often develop into a little tug followed by that exciting heavy pull.

One unforgettable time I landed fourteen barbel, all solid, hard-fighting fish but the largest was, as so many others, around the 6-lb mark. We were sure much larger fish swam the river, and came up with a theory as to why we had not caught one. As there was a much larger stock of average-sized fish, we thought that they found our baits first and were prepared to take them readily, while the larger, older and possibly wiser fish were more circumspect. Whether our theory was correct I shall never know, but the onus for failure was laid squarely on the barbel and not our lack of angling skills!

Reluctantly we left this delightful river, continuing our search for those elusive larger fish, to concentrate on the much harder, featureless and slow-flowing Yorkshire Ouse. Certainly the Ouse held some large barbel but they were relatively few and far between. One great difficulty faced us: finding one swim or even a stretch of the river containing these bigger fish. Gone were the shallows, the glides and the deeper pools. The Ouse was a typical lowland river: wide, deep and lacking in recognisable barbel swims. We sought advice from those who regularly fished it; we attended weekend fishing matches, again remembering the areas where a matchman had a barbel in his keepnet. After collating as much evidence as possible, we decided to base ourselves in the village of Dunsforth between Burrough-bridge and Aldwarke Bridge. Both the Swale and the Ure joined the Ouse in this area and it seemed a likely stretch to fish. While there were odd shallows, most of the Ouse had an even depth of at least 12 feet; it was a daunting prospect.

We knew we could spend hours fishing with not a barbel within hundreds of yards, and if we were lucky enough to find a barbel swim only the odd fish was likely to be present and it could take hour after hour of groundbaiting and fishing for just one bite. One the other hand, that bite could come from a huge fish so we were prepared to make the effort.

There was one other problem we hadn't bargained for: Tuppers Field which bordered the river. This field was notorious with match fishing anglers from Bradford, Leeds and York, who fished this section of the Ouse at weekends. Notorious, because of a hard-headed character called Tupper. Tupper was a large, evil-tempered ram. He did not take kindly to anglers, and if one was so foolhardy as to settle down on the river bank in

94

his field Tupper took immediate steps to remedy the matter. After a preliminary scoring of the earth with his front hooves, sending tufts of grass flying skyward, he put his great head, adorned with a fearsome set of curved horns, down, and charged.

Needless to say Tupper always kept the field to himself and his flock of ewes. Tupper's stretch was hardly fished, if ever, during his years of regal occupation.

I had by now acquired a small van which quickly became legendary with my angling friends for it was for ever racing up the A1 from Rotherham to Dunsforth.

I found yet another hospitable landlord and with such a pleasant base, I spent evenings, weekends and holidays trying to come to terms with this difficult river.

One holiday in late July I fished daily. For once the conditions were perfect. I found the river fining down nicely after an unseasonable rise due to a period of wet weather. With the possibility, even if it was remote, of hooking one of the great Ouse barbel I increased the strength of line and used slightly larger, hardened forged hooks. Another innovation was to employ a swimfeeder. This device—a weighted plastic tube about the size of a 35-mm film canister pierced with holes—was fixed to the end of the swivelled shot link, shots now being dispensed with. A swimfeeder can be open at either end, filled with maggots, luncheon meat or whatever and plugged with moistened breadbrumbs. Once on the river bed the breadcrumbs quickly wash away and the contents are released. For maggots only, a swimfeeder with closed ends is preferable, for the maggots crawl out of the holes rather than being released all together. So for many minutes a trickle of maggots can escape through the holes to trundle away down current. With this method of groundbaiting, the free offerings are released right by the baited hook.

In those days very few anglers, if any, were using swimfeeders when fishing the Ouse. My pioneering the method with some success soon became known and before long it became popular.

At the beginning of my holiday the river, though dropping down, was still flowing strongly, so I searched for a swim where the current was more gentle. I found some eight feet of water just beyond a bank of dense water weed that extended only a little from the margin. This deep swim, with moderate flow (far less than in mid-stream) and with the weeds giving cover so beloved by barbel, had many of the ingredients of a typical barbel swim. The more I studied the flow, the better I liked that spot. I would not

Chub and barbel swim on the River Wensum.

have been surprised to have found a notice board planted nearby with one word boldly printed on it—BARBEL!

I commenced feeding the swim with moistened breadcrumbs squeezed into balls liberally laced with maggots. Then, filling the feeder to the brim with maggots alone, I cast just beyond the weedbed nearby, so that I was fishing directly below the rod tip. Intuition allied to all the preceding years' experiences worked in harmony. Not only did that little area of water look promising but that promise was fulfilled. At times I had to wait patiently—often an hour or two without a tremble on the rod tip—every now and again reeling in, re-filling the feeder and then casting to a slightly different spot along the edge of the weeds.

During the whole of that holiday, fishing hard, I caught just five fish. However each fish was much larger than I had caught before, and the best was a magnificent specimen weighing 9 lb 4 oz; it proved to be one of the largest ever caught in that section of river.

The best swim I encountered was extremely difficult to fish. Difficult swims deter the average fisherman, so, because they are rarely disturbed, these areas often harbour the better fish.

The main problem was a line of piles, ancient stumps that had once shored up the river bank. These scarred and waterlogged stumps did not quite reach the surface and were situated a few feet out in the river. Naturally the piles would offer any hooked fish sanctuary and a barbel rushing between any of these obstructions would cause the line to snag against one of the piles. Then the abrasive surface could part the line as if it were drawn across a file.

While this swim was daunting to fish it was extremely comfortable to sit by due to the presence of a large tree trunk which we used to lean against, the natural conformation of which might have been designed for comfort; this swim was aptly termed the armchair.

Once a barbel was hooked, the fun began. Not only did they have to be held at first and lifted from the river bed, but they had to be persuaded to move out into mid-river. These tactics often succeeded, but inevitably some of the stronger fish were not to be bullied and seemed quite determined to swim among the piles. In fact as soon as they realised that they were in trouble they immediately charged through the stumps and in almost every case they gained their freedom.

This snag-ridden swim produced a series of good barbel. Mostly they averaged 5 lb or so and I had one beautifully-marked fish of over 6 lb. But in spite of its suitability as a good swim, I never connected with one of the really large Ouse barbel.

While concentrating my fishing time on this river I read an article in an angling magazine. This was written by Brian Morland, who described some of his experiences fishing for barbel on the upper reaches of the Ure. It was not long before we corresponded and eventually Brian was kind enough to invite Rob and me to join him and fish the river above Wensley.

The upper Ure is as unlike the Ouse as chalk to cheese. It is a clear, sparkling stream, chattering along over its gravelled shallows, piling up against mid-stream boulders, then sliding quiescent through the deeper glides and bends. The Ure is a typical northern trout stream holding a fine stock of native brown trout. In order to be allowed to fish we were obliged to become members of the angling club that controlled the water. Because of the trout, the club rules banned maggots as bait, and the fixed-spool reels that I had been using for years were also disallowed. I had to acquire a centre pin, basically the same design as the fishing reels that had been in use for centuries, but the contemporary versions constructed from modern materials were exceptionally free running, lightweight and a joy to handle. Having to revert to an up-to-date model of this old-fashioned reel in no way handicapped my fishing.

Luckily we were allowed to use worms as bait, and those Ure trout certainly took a liking to them. Even the largest, fattest lobworm was happily engulfed by even the little trout whose eyes were larger than their stomachs. All the trout we caught—and they were many—were carefully handled, unhooked and returned to the river.

To avoid the trout we tried our old well-proven baits of luncheon meat and sausage paste. Those capricious Ure barbel would have nothing whatsoever to do with these offerings, proving yet again the unpredictability inherent in the sport of angling.

For me the fascination lies in the fact that the more one learns the more there is to learn. In a lifetime's experience no one can do more than just scratch the surface; angling, like life itself, is always a challenge.

Fishing for the Ure barbel was a totally new experience. Not only did they show an interest in natural food and nothing else, but because of the water clarity, the fish could be clearly seen. As the sun rose after dawn and warmed the shallows, the barbel loved to move on to them. Using an eye shade and polarised sunglasses we watched as the fish moved out of the deeps and into the neck of a shallow or rippling glide, just inches deep. Their broad backs were clear of the water, wet and glistening as the slanting rays of sunlight burnished their bronzed scales. Triangular dorsal fins and the tips of deeply-forked scales waved and, tilting from side to side, looked for all the world like a fleet of tiny yachts tacking upwind. Such a sight was so intriguing that for some seconds all thought of trying to catch one of these barbel was forgotten. I just watched, completely fascinated, noting the impressive bow waves as each fish pushed onwards parting the current as it forged ahead.

We travelled with the minimum of tackle so that we could move upstream of the shoal then lay a trap. We tried to estimate the exact route that the barbel were likely to take, and having made a calculated decision, we cast a large lobworm with the mimimum of weight needed so that it would just hold bottom. Then we waited, nerves tingling with pent up excitement for the barbel to arrive. If our estimation was correct and it certainly wasn't on many an occasion, we would see a fish move even nearer to the bait, watch it pause, tilt and then move sideways, turning away downstream, the line lightening. Such fish hooked in the shallows rushed for the sanctuary of deeper water, making the rod bend in a full semi-circle, not just an arc, line singing like a ship's rigging in the wind.

The Ure was a stalking river, and with high banks we could stealthily creep from swim to swim. It took practise to spot a fish in the deeper glides. Often only an orange-toned fin or the end of a slowly waving tail protruding from a bank of weed denoted their presence.

The river scouring its course through sparsely-inhabited wild country was more like a highland stream, beguilingly gentle and placid, idly moving through the deeper runs and bends, but after rain, it would in a few hours rise bank high and the rushing torrent would gush seaward, roaring onward, the sound of turbulent water echoing down the vale.

The hill air was always pure and sweet, the slopes heather and bracken-clad; leaning willows and alders dipped their lower branches and brushed the surface. Black and white dippers flitted from rock to rock or plunged into the current, walking along the bottom searching the pebbles for insect larvae. The Ure valley was a land of enchantment. I was ever content casting my bait into some unexplored swim, wondering if by chance I had stumbled across the domain of some great fish. But it was not to be. I never caught a huge fish from that delightful river, but just as importantly, I did learn more about the habits of barbel and how to fish for them with growing confidence.

By 1975, much as I loved the Ure, the lure of bigger fish called me away to yet another barbel river—the Derwent. This river rises near Yelvington in North Yorkshire not far from Scarborough, runs west then turns south before joining the Ouse not far from where the Ouse empties into the Humber.

I decided to concentrate on the stretch of the Derwent near Stamford Bridge. Nearby was a weirpool. The fast-running, foaming, well-oxygenated water was beloved by barbel. Below the pool were beds of fine gravel, where the river was shallow, providing a fine spawning area. After this annual ritual was complete, the fish remained in these fast-running shallows to feed and clean themselves. Later the barbel fell back downstream, distributing themselves in the deeper glides and pools.

At the start of the season in June, the fish still frequented the shallow water so it was obvious that this section of the river gave me the best chance of contacting the shoals.

There were four excellent miles of water below Stamford to Kexby, and I often walked up to two miles to fish a favourite swim. I preferred the more remote areas, well away from any bridges and the more accessible points where anglers came to fish. Often, other anglers fished close to where they had parked their cars, so certain swims became heavily fished and the barbel, under constant pressure, either moved to safer pastures or became hook shy. I avoided these popular stretches therefore, like the plague.

The Stamford Bridge section of river was a classic barbel habitat: fast-running shallows, interspersed among quieter glides and deeper pools. These pools, some of them twelve feet deep, dark, mysterious, overhung by bank side trees, seemed timeless. Downstream of the shallow spawning sites below the weir, the swims were difficult to fish because of the densely wooded banks. Avoided by anglers, such stretches of river attract barbel who can go about their business undisturbed.

Rob and I walked the whole four miles of river checking depths and bottom features in those swims that we considered ought to hold a barbel shoal. After this preliminary work, we fished quite systematically, trying out one after another those swims that we decided were the most promising. I had discovered during our reconnaisance walks two swims, both snag-free and unencumbered with boulders, waterlogged tree branches and the conglomeration of debris that normally litters the bed of the deeper pools. On the opposite tree-lined bank, branches overhung the water. From the near bank a dense bed of waterweed protruded beyond which was clear water.

Our baits were the well-proven luncheon meat or maggots used with a swimfeeder and on this occasion, fishing alone, I carpeted the far edge of the weeds with maggots, then swung the baited hook and feeder brim full with lively wriggling 'goodies' so that they reached the bottom just beyond the weeds.

An elderly angler from Leeds, with whom I had passed the time of day earlier, was fishing another swim some little distance away.

I settled down holding the rod which was angled downstream across one knee, and keeping the tension to the weighted feeder. So I waited, sitting quite comfortably. The gentle murmur of running water and the sough of the breeze in the leaf-laden branches was soporific. I felt a slight lightening of the line which instantly awakened me from my daydream, and I concentrated my gaze on the rod tip. It seemed motionless, then, so suddenly that I was taken unawares, the tip pulled round savagely. Perhaps instinctively, I reacted by striking, but in a fleeting second, line was stripping off the reel as my unseen quarry surged away downstream. That barbel used the current. It presented its broad flank to the flow so that it could match the force exerted by a fully bent rod. Then, changing tactics the fish pressed its belly to the river bed and lay dormant. To try and put on more pressure in order to lift the barbel would have inevitably resulted in the comparatively light line breaking. So for a number of minutes, honours were even. The fish refused to move and I couldn't pressurise it to do so. The stalemate continued. Perhaps I should have eased the pressure, slackening the line in order that the fish might think it was free. But what I actually did was to maintain as heavy a pressure as I dared in the hope that I could eventually tire the fish so that it had to move.

After what seemed an eternity but in reality could only have been a minute or so, the barbel ran upstream passing me, then turned and fled downstream once again. Eventually the rapidly tiring fish circled deep down under the rod tip, after one last plunge which must have drained it of all energy. I finally coaxed it to the surface and the waiting landing net.

That barbel was large and with some trepidation, hoping against hope that I had secured my long-awaited ten pounder, I set about removing the hook and prepared the weighing scales.

The ancient angler who had seen all the commotion arrived and was able to witness the needle register 10 lb 4 oz. I had done it at last. All the disappointments, the frustration and even self-doubt were forgotten. We both gazed down at what was one of the biggest Yorkshire barbel ever caught. That should have been enough excitement for anyone but triumph very nearly turned to tragedy.

Unnoticed, while I played the fish a shooting party had spaced themselves along the opposite bank, awaiting any game driven towards them by the line of beaters working the nearby fields, copses and hedgerows.

Soon a stream of pheasants passed over the guns and as we watched, one bird flew straight towards us, so fast that it seemed to take the guns by surprise. But as it flew low across the river, one of the shooters turned round and aimed. Instinctively I threw the old angler down, sprawling on top of him, as two shots were fired. I heard quite clearly the hiss of the pellets passing just above us. It was terrifying, we lay pressed flat on the ground for some time before we dared move. Then cautiously raising our heads, we saw a group of guns crowded around the culprit voicing their displeasure at his irresponsible behaviour. One of the party called across. After informing him that we were not harmed, he apologised at length. The old angler, Stan, was very shaken and I too was shocked, but we were alive, unhurt. Still, the memory of how we could so easily have been killed remains with me to this day.

Within a few years I had left Yorkshire. I had obtained a transfer to British Rail in East Anglia and decided to live in Norwich, central to all the fine fishing that Norfolk offered. I soon came to love Norfolk which was so different from the Yorkshire vales with its gentle well-wooded, rolling countryside, not as flat as is generally believed and harbouring a wealth of waters—waters varying in character from the Broads, slow flowing rivers, ancient estate lakes adjacent to great houses and a host of more recently excavated gravel pits. It seemed too good to be true and perhaps what excited me most was the proximity of the delightful Wensum, which was reputed to hold barbel even bigger than my Derwent fish.

The gentle, clear-running Wensum has carved its way, at first through primeval forest, then as flood after flood eroded the bordering land, its own flood plain, now water meadows enriched with silt. Here cattle graze, long-billed snipe probe the water-logged fields in winter and sickle-winged wildfowl from far northern tundras whistle down the north east winds.

The Wensum is steeped in history. It has borne the Saxon and Viking longboats; the power of its waters have turned the water wheels since Roman times. Through flint and pantiled villages the river twists and turns, villages still linked to their ancient past by place names ending in -by, -thorpe or -twaite, denoting the original settlements.

There is relatively higher ground to the west of the county of Norfolk—a chalk ridge—a natural watershed whence short streams flow west to the Great Ouse and Wash, while the longer Wensum flows in the opposite direction. It rises by the Raynhams, a clear rippling trickle, slowly widening and deepening as it flows north, then turning east in a great loop to reach the market town of Fakenham and thereafter south, through the centre of Norwich, eventually to lose its identity by joining the Yare.

The indigenous fish inhabiting the Wensum were roach, dace, perch, bream, pike, brown trout and lesser species such as minnows, bull heads and loach. Once it was full of those miniature freshwater lobsters the crayfish. Crayfish only thrive in pure, unpolluted running water and their numbers have dwindled. But some of the native brown trout remain boosted by a series of stockings. There are some large trout still be be found in the millpools, mostly privately owned, where they have become carnivorous, fattening on the little dace, roach and minnows.

In 1955 the water authority obtained 100 chub from tributaries of the Wye. These were released downstream of Hellesdon Mill on the northern outskirts of Norwich and as an experiment just 26 barbel were also introduced. In 1972 a further 98 barbel were stocked, and the river has suited both species, in particular chub, who have thrived.

While the barbel took longer to establish themselves they have settled down well, found the river to their liking and have spawned successfully. Provided some massive pollution does not ruin this beautiful river, its reputation as the home of record-breaking barbel is assured.

While the Wensum has been spared industrial pollution, it is alas, as so many of our running waters, a river in slow decline. Flowing through the granary of England, Wensum water is abstracted not only for household use but to water fields. In an area of intensive agriculture, excessive use of nitrogenous fertiliser has seen an annual leach from the soil into the rivers. This, added to phosphates from sewage has over-fertilised the river leading to massive weed proliferation. The once-clear Wensum, now in times of drought, is reduced to almost the status of a still water so minimal is the flow. It can also be affected by algae colonisation due to the same cause: excess fertiliser. Farmers are always pressing the water authority to get surplus water down river as fast as possible. The growth of weeds in summer holds the water back, so the drainage engineers do their drastic weedcutting just at the time when the weeds are sheltering all the fry that result from the spawning of many species including barbel.

Drainage engineers seem to be totally ignorant of river ecology and it took many years of intense pressure from Norfolk anglers to persuade them to carry out their weedcutting in a more responsible manner. Now at least they leave a fringe of bankside weedbeds, concentrating on the middle section to provide a channel for unrestricted waterflow. Having eradicated one danger that was destroying fish life, slowly but surely, yet another disaster befell the river. A large chemical works on the outskirts of Norwich had so polluted its environment that there was a real danger that the pollutants could seep into the river and poison the Norwich water supply. As the city's water was abstracted downstream of this possible seepage, a whole abstraction works is being sited well away from the chemical works upstream. Thankfully Norwich water will remain safe but the new scheme will drastically affect the flow of water in that part of the Wensum that holds most of the barbel and certainly those very few really large fish that are known to exist.

This book is not the place to apportion blame but we Norfolk anglers cannot understand just why the chemical works were sited alongside the river in the first place.

However, when I came to Norfolk, this event was unforeseen and I spent much of my first year exploring not only still waters but the Wensum upstream of Norwich and in particular the known barbel stretch. As the river is normally clear I could see the character of likely-looking swims as well as spotting individual fish. I had spent years learning exactly what constituted a good barbel swim in Yorkshire and this hard-won knowledge stood me in good stead.

I fished occasionally but my limited time had to be divided between the river and fishing for other species. Unlike some, I am not a 'one fish' man, each new water and each new species is a challenge I cannot resist. During that first season I caught some average-sized fish which whetted my appetite, and I resolved to spend more time barbel fishing in the following year.

There were problems to frustrate my ambition which was to land a huge Wensum fish. The Wensum is not wide, and because it is often exceptionally clear it needed great stealth and much creeping and crawling to spot fish at all. I soon discovered that the big barbel seemed to possess a sixth sense and could detect my presence however careful my stalking. Apart from these difficulties, the river was heavily weeded, making it impossible to cast a bait into a clear run. Baits lost in a jungle of weed are unlikely to be easily found, and a weed-festooned bait catches few fish.

I felt that my best chance of success was to concentrate on the more inaccessible parts of the river, those heavily weeded and masked by overhanging trees and shrubs. These almost unfishable swims were quite certain to be ignored by all but the most dedicated of anglers. The barbel who naturally gravitate to the well-bushed banks which provide them with cover overhead and security, would respond to baits with far more confidence than in the more open areas which they had learnt could spell danger.

As there were few clear runs between the weeds I had no option but to wade in and pull out weed in order to expose the gravel as well as removing quantities of waterlogged branches which could have inhibited playing any large fish. Once a number of areas had been cleared—a wet and tedious task—I pre-baited these with sweetcorn and cooked hempseed. Hemp attracts fish. They seem to love it and barbel are no exception. As for the sweetcorn, this has been proved to be an excellent bait also and needs no preparation, it is used direct from the can.

At the beginning of the season I discovered a shoal of barbel that spent

most of their time in six feet of water directly below the dense overhanging branches of a pair of willows. There were possibly a dozen fish, most of good average size with one or two very much larger.

This was a really difficult swim to come to terms with. There was nowhere to sit or crouch in comfort and without slight modification it was impossible to place the bait where I wished. I cleared an opening in the tangle of twigs, just large enough to pass my rod through then lower the bait right into the barbel's domain. The only way I could sit in order to do this was to straddle one of the large bankside branches.

On the evening of June 15th I baited the swim, then waited impatiently for midnight when the fishing season commenced. Because of the darkness this made for extremely difficult fishing. Every movement had to be careful and deliberate, it was so easy to get the rod trapped in the tree branches. Slowly, and with infinite care, the rod was passed through without incident and the baited hook allowed to drop down into the water

and sink to the river bed. Cramped and uncomfortable I waited, buoyed up with expectancy, but for some time nothing happened and I began to wonder if the barbel had moved off in the darkness to feed elsewhere.

Then so suddenly that it took me completely by surprise, the rod slammed round and I was playing a barbel that after a spirited performance was netted. I had already made sure that it was possible to get the large spread landing net into position before me.

So my first Wensum barbel that season was a respectable fish of 6 lb. Once the commotion had died down a shoal of chub found the ground bait. I suffered a succession of these followed by an infestation of eels. That ruined any chance of another barbel because those eels grabbed every bait as soon as it reached the bottom.

As daylight crept across the valley, and the sun rose, the eels departed, but no more bites were forthcoming. I even began to hope for an obliging chub to break the monotony. It must have been nearing 10 am. I had been watching the bottom of the swim and could even see my hookbait clearly, when suddenly—as if materialising from nowhere—I noticed the streamlined shape of a much larger barbel, like a shadow, its tail slowly waving from side to side. It inspected the few remnants of ground bait, sidled up to the hookbait, took it immediately then turned away downstream. I struck and had the rod nearly ripped from my hand. That barbel decided to put as much distance as possible between itself and the willows. It fled, and I had to release yard after yard of line. Eventually the power exerted by a fully bent rod began to tell, and perhaps to ease the strain, the fish turned and ploughed upstream. Keeping as much pressure on the fish as I dared I endeavoured to steer it towards the sunken landing net. Perhaps it saw me, but this barbel found its second wind and tore off downstream once again.

As I was bringing the fish back for the second time, the line went slack and the barbel was free. Sick with disappointment, I checked the hook which had been new and made of forged carbon steel. It had opened wide. Now it takes a great deal of force to open the bend of such a hook and I began to wonder just how large that barbel really was.

Eventually I hooked another good fish and unbelievably the new hook opened out in exactly the same fashion. This was the first occasion that I had tried out this particular pattern, which had been recommended by a friend. Needless to say nothing would have persuaded me to use that type of hook again.

It was not long before I began to realise that catching Wensum barbel and the large ones in particular, was going to be no easy task. Unlike the Yorkshire rivers, the Wensum's normal clarity and its comparative narrowness, presented problems that I had not encountered. It was all too apparent that the sight of the line or the barely discernible splash of a delicately cast bait 'put the fish down' as anglers say. Those barbel seem to equate such events with danger and as a result they become nervous, refusing to feed often for many hours. I pondered the problem and came to a decision: I should have to fish during the dark hours, suffering chub and those infernal eels if need be.

I had discovered over the years that the barbel's daytime lies were often vacated during darkness and that the fish moved to other swims to forage. Barbel seemed to gain confidence as the light faded, then they were prepared to leave those swims shaded by dense overhanging vegetation. A pattern of feeding also emerged, the fish fed avidly during the first hours of the night, followed by a lull and then came on the feed just before dawn. As the light increased, feeding became more desultory before the barbel returned to their day-time swims.

To discover these night-time feeding areas I walked the river bank both up and down stream of the known day-time swims, noting likely areas which could be pre-baited, then fished in darkness.

The twin-willow barbel swim, good as it proved to be, was a headache. One night I hooked yet another big fish that ran downstream close to the bank and the line became firmly lodged in the branches. I could neither free the line nor retrieve any of it and the barbel was in much the same predicament, it couldn't take more line and so became tethered.

I'm still not sure why the line did not part, but it did not, and in order to free the line some desperate measures were required. Grabbing the net, I forced my way through the thicket and waded into the river. Close to the bank the water was about five feet deep but to get round both trees, I had to venture further out. I tentatively stepped forward and found myself out of my depth. Alone at night, this was a dangerous situation but somehow, clutching rod and net, I floundered past the trees and with immense effort reached more shallow water. Climbing up the bank was a nightmare but with the line now cleared, I managed to regain contact with what had been a remarkably docile fish. After a minute or so I netted a beautiful barbel of 9 lb 4 oz. I continued the quest for the much larger fish that I had seen in this stretch of river. In spite of the problems I still felt that the tree swim would produce one of these monster barbel. But as the days passed, they eluded all my scheming.

One very early morning in July, the meadows wet with dew and the river running a little faster than usual, fining down after rain, I was once more perched precariously on the willow branch. I lowered some groundbait by using a bait dropper—a device that opens when it reaches the bottom and releases its contents.

I sat quietly enjoying the peace of a summer morning, small birds settled in the branches, unaware of my presence, chattering and flitting from branch to branch. Every now and again I heard the heavy splashes caused by rising fishing and momentarily forgot the discomfort of the hard willow branch by watching a dragonfly hovering like a winged aquamarine jewel, then darting forward every few seconds, its reflection mirrored in the stream.

The slight tension of the line, held by finger and thumb, and vibrated minutely by the current was my only communication with the baited hook. Time passed. Two mallard following the river's course chuckled overhead and just as I shifted my position carefully, to ease an aching leg, the line tightened, giving me a split-second warning before the rod tip jagged round hard. I sensed that I had hooked a good fish, which like all the fish hooked by the willows raced away downstream, thumping the rod tip as though it was being struck by a sandbag. Any fish downstream of an angler can use the current to its great advantage, by turning broadside on to the stream it can add extra pressure on the line, which does not diminish but rather increases as the angler endeavours to play it back.

I always try to get my fish to swim upstream, then the current acts to my advantage as the fish has to fight the flow of water as well as the line pressure. Sometimes a slight steady pressure will persuade a fish to turn, then, provided that light but steady strain is maintained it will force upstream. Once past, it is possible to apply maximum force hoping to bring the fish up to the surface. This seems to disorientate it and it will thrash wildly. Before it can regain equilibrium, steady pressure plus the effect of the current will bring the fish in quite easily. By these tactics the fish is hauled downstream towards the well-sunk net. Very often the fish, on seeing the soft green meshes, takes it for a bed of weed and dashes headlong into the folds. So it happened on this occasion, I laid the net down on the grass and parted the mesh to behold my biggest everv barbel of 11 lb 12 oz. The willow tree swim had come up trumps at last.

During the remaining summer months and through the early autumn I caught many Wensum barbel including two more over 10 lb. The river was yielding up its secrets. It was hard work and hard fishing but I had caught more big barbel than in all my years on the Yorkshire rivers, and from a river that did not hold one two decades ago.

Few anglers bother to fish barbel during the winter. It has been understood that cold water turns them sluggish which is certainly the case, but in a mild spell of warmer winds from the south-west when the water temperature rises, they do feed for short periods.

I was still determined to catch one of the monsters so I decided that whenever I considered conditions suitable I would fish. At least I wouldn't have to compete for swims with the other barbel anglers, although there would still be those fishing for the obliging chub, a species that can tolerate and feed in the coldest weather. I was well aware that once the water temperature rises to 40 °F barbel will feed and if it rises to 45 °F I become really confident.

For many a month temperatures remained cold. Christmas came and I departed north for a short holiday. It had rained heavily while I was away but the cold spell was over and once back in Norfolk the air felt balmy, a foretaste of spring not usually expected until early April.

Because my home was close to the river I could check on water flow both before and after work. I saw that the Wensum was high, very coloured with suspended sediment, but quite definitely dropping when I assessed water conditions on my return. As I was still on holiday I decided to fetch my rod and fish for an hour or two. Neil accompanied me. Selecting a swim that I considered ideal for the conditions, some seven to eight feet deep that was just below a wooded stretch of river where the current had undercut one bank, I settled down.

I introduced some cubes of luncheon meat as well as balls of sausage paste, so that they would be trundled through the swim by the current. The hook bait was cast out and I settled down to await developments. I felt confident and this confidence was rewarded with a barbel of 6 lb followed by a fine 4-lb chub. Then all went quiet and although I continued fishing until darkness fell I did not have a single bite.

The next day was still mild, but even better the river had fallen steadily during the night and cleared considerably. I doubted if such conditions could prevail for long and decided that if I was going to catch one of the huge barbel that season it had to be now or never.

At 3 pm I was back at the river, using the same baits and fishing once again in the swim below the copse.

After twenty minutes or so, I felt a tentative pull on the rod tip immediately followed by a surge of power transmitted by the line. The rod bent and bent; no doubt about it I just knew I had hooked an enormous fish. This fish, like its predecessors raced downstream. It ignored a mass of snags by an overhanging tree, and I managed to turn it with the line taut as a bowstring. Soon the barbel was close in below the rod but it hugged the bottom tenaciously and it was some moments before a huge head broke surface and I slid the fish towards the net that Neil had sunk in anticipation. Dexterously, Neil enfolded the fish and we lifted ashore the biggest barbel I had ever seen. It was stupendous, in length and girth unbelievable and it made my 10-lb fish look small fry. That barbel proved to be the largest ever caught in the Wensum—a Wensum record—all 13 lb 2 oz of magnificent fish.

I suppose I should have been satisfied, perhaps I should have rested content and turned my attention to other species. But I had seen even larger fish and I just could not resist the challenge to try and catch one of them.

Then the bitter northerly wind arrived; gathering snow-laden clouds over Arctic regions, it seared Norfolk with such frosts that the fields became iron hard and sprinkled with snow.

By early March, with only a few days of the fishing season remaining, the first breath of spring softened the penetrating cold and the temperature began to rise.

When I reached the river I found many of my favourite swims occupied by anglers making the most of the few days left. It seemed as if these anglers, not being able to fish for weeks were determined to have a last fling before fishing had to cease until June.

I had to wander the bank looking for a likely swim and to add to my troubles I sensed a chill creeping down the valley; the milder weather would not last much longer.

I had taken along Derrick Amies. Derrick has caught more 30-lb pike than any other angler but he had never caught a barbel. He had by now become a partner in my tackle business. I suppose my obsession to land a big Wensum barbel had rubbed off on him, or perhaps he felt if he encouraged me enough and came along to help me I would concentrate more on the business and less on barbel!

The light had begun to fade before I found an unoccupied swim, a stretch where the current flowed a little faster but where I had caught barbel before.

After two hours not one bite had registered. It was by now dark. Then, an extremely obliging chub, a fair fish of 3 lb was caught and returned. I fished on and almost at once I hooked a barbel that weighed a little under 8 lb. It was quite a tussle landing that fish, hampered by the relentless flow of water pushing through the swim and the pitch darkness.

As we examined the fish by torchlight Derrick was as thrilled and fascinated as if had caught it himself. We decided in spite of the lateness of the hour and the increasing cold to continue fishing.

Just twenty minutes later I was playing a fish that I instinctively knew could be the fish of a lifetime. It is easy to overestimate the possible size of a fish when it is being played in total darkness. The fast water too would only place more strain on the line so I handled this fish as carefully as possible. This barbel had no intention of leaving the river bed. For some time it clamped its belly to the bottom, close by. As I coaxed it to the surface Derrick made a heroic effort to net the fish but failed. Stirred into activity, the barbel tore off downstream taking full advantage of the current. This time Derrick followed my instructions to the letter, he stretched forward and sank the net as far out from the bank as he could, no easy task with the current pushing hard against the meshes. He waited as I raised the fish to the surface and pressurised it back upstream. It was touch and go. How the line didn't part I shall never know. Derrick made no mistakes; once the net and fish were safely on the grassy bank I flicked on the torch. At once I recognised my 13-lb fish, as immaculate as ever, and noted with delight that it was four ounces heavier than before, scaling 13 lb 6 oz. Derrick gazed in awe at this magnificent barbel whose golden scales shone wet and dazzling in the torch light.

To have continued fishing would have been an anticlimax, besides I felt tired, elated but desperately drained. We slipped the fish into the cold dark depths of the river and trudged back to the car saying little. The following spring I was presented with the National Association of Specialist Anglers' award for the largest barbel caught in England during that particular season, a plaque I shall always cherish. The gentle Wensum may hold even larger fish, it certainly did at that time. Not only did I glimpse the odd enormous barbel but on two occasions I hooked massive fish, only to lose them. It is quite possible that one or two huge barbel still exist in that peaceful river, and it is not beyond the bounds of possibility that one day the sparkling Wensum may produce the record barbel. If it does I for one will not be too surprised.

A winter chub angler on an Oxfordshire stream.

Chub: That 'Fearfullest of Fishes'

'The cheven, chavender or chub' is how that loquacious angler Walton, referred to the fish that today is universally termed the chub—although the cheven (now spelt chevin) is still used by some contemporary fishermen as a form of endearment when speaking of that 'fearfullest of fishes' to quote Walton yet again.

Chub, perhaps an abbreviation of chubby, aptly describes a fish which is thickset, broad shouldered and blunt headed. If ever there was a fish-shaped fish, the chub is it. It is bold of eye with a large-scaled back and flanks that shine like polished brass. While most chub seem to weigh about $2^1/2$ to 3 lb, the largest ever caught by an angler in Britain is over 7 lb and it is almost certain that heavier fish exist.

Seemingly ever hungry, chub will take bait when other fish are reduced to lying on the river bed torpid with cold. Bright sunny weather that sends tench seeking the shadows draw the chub to the surface to sunbathe like carp. The chub is an aggressive species that exploits to the full the food sources within its environment, so catholic in its taste that it will sample any object remotely edible. Here the chub is helped by being both a carnivore and herbivore, happy to eat blackberries that fall from the brambles into the water, whilst many a Victorian angler caught his chub on cherries. No fish has such a penchant for cheese, and while cheddar will suffice, chub have a weakness for Danish Blue and Stilton, though I imagine only very wealthy anglers are prepared to scatter cubes of Stilton on the water for gourmet chub.

A chub would barter his soul for a large, black, orange-bellied slug, takes kindly to bread in all its forms, is fond of maggots, adores large worms and goes potty over wasp grubs which are on a par with slugs. In addition to these, sweetcorn, luncheon meat, sausage and liver pate are relished—and any little fish had better look to his future when a hungry chub is on the prowl! Hard-shelled, freshwater crayfish are just grist to their mill; a chub can pulverise a crayfish with its powerful pharyngeal teeth which are located in its throat. Only the most foolish angler, when endeavouring to remove the hook from a deep-hooked chub, would push his finger well inside its mouth. Having a finger trapped in a car door would do less damage!

If it seems strange that Walton termed the chub the 'fearfullest of fishes', it is because he was writing about their wariness and of their being fearful, rather than their being frightening. A swallow skimming low along the river will send surface-feeding chub down to the bottom; likewise the slightest movement on the riverbank, or the vibration of a football being kicked in an adjacent field, will also stop them feeding. Chub only flee when imminent danger threatens, but when their suspicions have been aroused there is no stopping them—they fade away like grey ghosts gliding through cloisters. Once disturbed, chub take some little time to regain their confidence and the bigger, older and wiser the chub, the more circumspect and wary it becomes. An hour for every pound has often been quoted, but even if that is a bit of an exaggeration, you should expect to wait an hour or two for a scared chub to regain confidence.

Chub are river fish; they are at home in running water—but when introduced to, or if they find their way into still water, they still seem to thrive and maintain a rapid rate of growth. In fact large lake chub tend to be more difficult to catch on rod and line than their counterparts in rivers, and appear to develop pronounced predatory tendencies. In the smaller rivers a chub swim is easy enough to locate because except when foraging in open water, they lie up in the most inaccessible places, often choosing the quieter, deeper water close by a tangle of tree roots.

Any deepish pool where vegetation spreads umbrella-like, shading the water, will provide a home for a chub or two. So will rafts of debris; even the smallest will as often as not shelter just one large fish. Such insignificant lies can be overlooked by the casual angler. Even a steep bank, with brambles, nettles or willowherb growing by the water's edge will give a chub some sense of security; in such a situation a chub will lie in quite shallow water only inches from the bank. In summer when the ranunculus and streamer weed are lush and thick, these too shelter chub as well as providing a well-stocked larder of insects and crustacia.

If chub swims are easy to detect, presenting a bait among such a jungle of snags is quite a different matter. Provided the angler's presence has not been sensed, and the bait can be cast with pin-point accuracy into such places, it will almost certainly be taken. But the commotion caused by extracting a hooked fish from such a swim will undoubtedly spook other chub in the vicinity. Then it may take hours for those fish to settle down and become catchable.

A 5lb 5-oz winter chub from the River Wensum, taken on legered
breadflake.

My personal best chub from the River Wensum: 5lb 10oz.

When a large chub has some smaller fish sharing its domain, it is always difficult to catch. The small fish seem to be quicker off the mark, or perhaps the larger far more wary chub likes his juniors to do a little tasting in order to ascertain how safe is the largesse that has suddenly appeared.

Vic Bellars has told me of a shoal of chub that lived in a deep pool in a little Norfolk river. That shoal comprised six fish. The smallest weighed $2^1/2$ lb while two of the largest were over 6 lb. Vic spent many hours on his stomach, hidden by the tall grasses, observing these fish. The smallest lay at the head of the shoal which faced the gentle current; this fish was the most active, and regularly quartered the river bed. The next two, lying further back occasionally moved out of line to inspect some suspected food item that drifted into the pool. But the larger fish remained on station at the rear seemingly uninterested in the activities of their shoal mates.

Vic fished hard trying to catch one of the huge chub. Positioning himself downstream he cast his bait so that it sank to lie on the bottom just astern of the two big fish. Without exception the smallest fish found the bait. Vic caught the $2^1/2$ pounder so many times it became embarrassing. That fish had to go, and the next time Vic fished he took a large plastic bucket. Sure enough the little fish obliged and was taken for a long walk, at least half a mile, until Vic found what he thought would provide an excellent home for that greedy fish. Three days later he caught it again, it had come back!

Vic never did manage to catch either of the two big chub, but night fishing with small deadbait accounted for number four in the shoal, a fine fish just one ounce under 5 lb. This only goes to prove that even when large chub have been located the problem of hooking them can sometimes seem insoluble.

When chub are holed up in the most inaccessible swims such as those situated under overhanging vegetation that touches the water, most anglers pass by considering such places impossible to fish. But a bait can be winkled into such a fastness as I shall describe. It is done by the use of PVA string or tape. This product dissolves quickly when immersed in water. The hook—normally some 12 to 18 inches long—is made much longer—even to as much as 4 or 5 feet. The baited hook is doubled back up the line and secured with a turn or two of PVA. If the weight is cast so that it drops right up against the branches and sinks to the bottom, within a few seconds the PVA dissolves and the bait is free to be trundled by the current right into the chub's holt. Usually the fish respond almost instantly and the bite is savage, slamming the rod tip round. Then things become more difficult as the large powerful fish has to be hauled away before it can bolt for cover in the mass of snags which such swims are always endowed with.

When the branches do not brush the surface, the bait can be hitched to something that floats—a short piece of balsa wood for example. Sitting upstream of the tree, the balsa raft can be floated right under the branches and held there. As the PVA dissolves, the bait falls away and sinks. It's easy when you know how, but even some experienced chub anglers seem unaware of such ploys.

Naturally, for these methods to work, there must be enough current to carry the bait along the bottom and the bait should be a neutrally weighted and buoyant one, such as a bread flake. Large lugworms if a little air is injected into the head section, are a particularly good bait, but heavy baits such as cheese paste or crayfish need a more powerful current to move them.

But there are times when the chub leave their sanctuary and then the angler has the odds stacked in his favour. During the dark hours and in the half light of dawn and dusk the chub emerge to hunt. Then the fish will patrol the river both upstream and downstream of their home. When the water is running clear the fish can be seen with the naked eye, but polarizing glasses which eliminate surface glare (particularly those with yellow lenses) are essential if the fish are to be seen clearly. Such fish actively seeking food are easy enough to catch but may not necessarily be the largest as you are likely to encounter the same problem that confronted Vic: the smaller fish nearly always get the bait first. Sometimes the only way to catch the better fish is to wait patiently with the bait on the hook, then when the large chub drifts away from its companions a bait can be cast in its vicinity. Another trick is to cast a freelined slug so that it plops into the water just behind a chub's tail. The fish will react in one of

Winter dawn on the River Wensum, settled in a chub swim.

two ways: either it will turn in a flash and perhaps instinctively engulf the bait, or it will flee; one never knows.

I knew very little about chub and certainly nothing of such techniques when I first became interested in fishing for them. When I was a boy, the distance I could travel, (except for the Sunday coach trips with my father) was restricted to how far I could travel on my bicycle. But this did give me access to the river Ryton, 12 miles away. This pretty little stream ran clear, twisting and turning through the countryside, the water deepening on the bends. It was a change to fish in open countryside after the canals and stillwaters that ran close by the factories of my home town of Rotherham; the rippling Ryton demanded very different techniques from those grey waters.

While my friend and I fished for roach and dace we occasionally spotted much larger specimens than we ever caught. These were chub; they were not numerous nor even large—perhaps a 3-lb fish would have been a monster for the river. Naturally we tried to catch what seemed to us to be a very large fish indeed, but it was many a day before we succeeded. We were quite ignorant in the ways of chub and no doubt did not move stealthily enough. Small boys are forever fidgeting, walking or perhaps even running along the bank and the chub must have been aware of us long before we started to fish for them.

The more difficult the fish is to catch the more determined I am to keep trying, and even at that tender age I refused to accept failure. The roach and dace were not all that easy to catch either, but those chub were a challenge. I asked advice from mature anglers, including my father, and sought advice from books too—losing all interest for a while in the roach. We float-fished for these with maggots and as no chub had fallen for these I felt that a new bait, one that would have irresistible appeal to a fat chub had to be found.

The books extolled the efficacy of cheese paste, and soon I learned how to make it. Taking some stale white bread without the crust, I soaked it in water, then twisted it in a clean cloth until most of the water was expelled. The resultant paste was kneaded until not a lump remained, then a little at a time, grated cheese was worked into the mix. Enough was added until the smooth paste smelt decidedly cheesy. I also discovered that the addition of custard powder would turn the bait an attractive yellow.

Concentrating on those parts of the river where I had seen most chub, I fished in the simplest way possible. I used a hook (larger than those I had used to catch roach and dace), and knotted the end of the line; the float and weight were dispensed with. This method is called freelining. The marble-sized ball of cheese paste had sufficient weight to cast quite a way and was dense enough to sink quickly.

I would sit on the riverbank upstream of one of the deeper holes, throw in some balls of bait and then cast the bait so it came to rest on the bottom in the same area. Then holding the rod with the line not quite tightened to the bait, I waited, praying that a chub would smell the baits, find the free samples, eat a couple, then finding them not only palatable but safe, would take the bait as well. Eventually, one not-to-be forgotten day the line lightened, the rod tip jagged, and I hooked my first ever chub. It was not that big, certainly not one of the few three pounders, but it was far larger than the roach or dace I usually caught. Catching that fish was exciting enough, but it was the thinking, the research and the effort I had put into it that made it so memorable. That chub was a prize to be cherished, and reluctantly I'm sure, I returned it to the river where it swam off to some shaded holt where it could sulk for an hour or two undisturbed.

As I have mentioned cheese paste is a good bait in winter. Unlike cubes of cheese which chub are also fond of, it does not harden in cold water, and therefore hooking a fish is easier. In spite of all the vast array of boilie baits designed to catch carp (and the chub can be caught on these), plain old-fashioned cheese paste remains a fine chub bait which I still use today.

During my latter years fishing the Lincolnshire Bain, I discovered a stretch of river, upstream of where we normally fished for roach that teemed with chub. Their average weight seemed to be greater than that of the fish in the little Ryton and certainly there were few very large fish living in that part of the river. It was on this section that I learned other techniques with which to outwit some of the bigger fish.

I now owned a quiver-tip rod. This had a fine flexible tip spliced into the end of the rod. It would magnify the most delicate of bites, bites that would have been undetectable on a normal rod. In really cold water even so hardy a fish as a chub becomes soporific; its metabolism changes. Unlike most other fish faced with extremes of cold however, chub will still take a bait provided they do not have to move far to obtain it. When they do, the bite is often so gentle that it hardly registers on a normal rod tip. As for the bait, it needs to lie still rather than be waving from side to side, and it should be smaller than would be normal in summer.

The Bain chub were fond of bread flake, and also small cubes of crust. Crust is very buoyant and a particularly good bait in winter when presented so that it rises a few inches off the bottom and just wobbles in the current. The anchoring weight is naturally set very close to the bait so as to prevent it floating upward too far. Cheese paste in which I had so much faith did not really interest those Lincolnshire chub—nor surprisingly did lobworms. It remains unexplained why chub in certain rivers will take one bait while those in another do not take to them so readily.

During very mild weather the chub of the Bain could be caught on pieces of crust floating on the surface just as the carp could at Ravensfield Ponds. Like the carp, the chub would not suck down a crust if they could see the line floating in the surface film. The last few inches of line had to be ungreased so that it would sink. Surface crust fishing is one of the most exciting ways of catching chub. Finding a promising length of river, I would throw in a few crusts and as they drifted, would watch their progress. Sometimes they would just float away until lost from view. But sometimes a swirling rise would break the surface as one of the crusts disappeared. This was the signal to introduce a couple more followed by a crust on my hook. This had to drift down with the others at exactly the same speed. If it dragged, so making a wake, the chub were sure to notice and have nothing to do with that particular crust. But if the line was well greased so that it floated, and the reel bale arm was opened, the crust would be carried downstream by the current quite naturally. Crust fishing is quite fascinating, I would keep my eyes glued on my crust, and as it entered the area where some of the free offerings had been taken, the tension would become heightened and well nigh unbearable. Another large swirl and the crust would be gone, then I had to steal myself to wait for the chub to turn down, usually only a second or two. Then, and not before, I would trap the line against the reel spool with my finger and sweep the rod back to set the hook. Occasionally a second fish could be caught from the same swim, but more normally playing a fish, even if it could be hustled away from its fellows was enough to put any other chub down. They seemed to know instinctively that the crusts were not what they seemed. But there were always other swims and other chub, and when fishing with floating crust I often walked for miles.

The lower reaches of the Bain upstream of its junction with the Witham, where the current ran more slowly, contained much larger chub than could be found elsewhere in the river, but still the biggest fish seemed to elude all my efforts. My best ever from the pleasant stream was a fine fish of 4 lb 2 oz.

I have already written of the wild, beautiful Yorkshire rivers where I spent years in search of large barbel, but when the barbel became nearly impossible to catch during the winter months, Rob Weldon (who was also a member of the Yorkshire Specimen Group) and I used to spend much of our fishing time chasing chub.

The Swale which I have mentioned with its rippling glides and mysterious pools was always a joy to fish. There were plenty of chub but they were generally rather small, with a few fish averaging 3 to 4 lb. Much later, when I had left Yorkshire for Norfolk, I learnt that the Swale chub seemed to have thrived and there were rumours of a 6-lb fish that had been caught from the river.

Where the Swale joins the Lower Ure, the latter eventually becoming the Ouse, was the section of river that I preferred to fish. These spate rivers were never at the same level for more than a day or two. Within hours the Swale could carry an extra twelve feet of water becoming an unfishable, soupy, foam-flecked, raging torrent. It was frustrating as well as expensive to drive 70 miles to fish, only to find it was impossible, so before setting out I used to ring Bob who lived near enough to the river to keep an eye on conditions. Usually this worked well enough, but we were occasionally caught out—especially if it had been raining over the hills near the source. This excess water would rush downstream, swelling the river in places where there hadn't been a drop of rain, making predicting water levels hazardous.

Nevertheless, we welcomed the first of the winter floods which swept away the rotting water weeds and the lesser snags like the small branches and brushwood and scoured the river bed so that it was easier to fish. As always, when the floods subsided and the water cleared, the fishing was at its very best. In spite of all my efforts I never landed my longed-for 5-lb chub, but I came near with a wonderfully conditioned fish of 4 lb 14^1/2 oz.

As for the Ouse, where undoubtedly 5-lb chub lived, I failed there too. The river was so coloured, wide and deep, that a recognisable chub swim did not exist. All we could do was search for variations in bottom structure in deep near-bank swims on bends with overhanging vegetation. When the current was not too fierce, we fished well out in the middle of the river, where once again we preferred to cast our baits to where there was at least some variation of depth such as a ridge or deeper trough. To cope with the flow, a whole string of heavy swan shot had to be attached to the link, often as many as six. We even used weights of 1^1/2 oz at times.

This part of the Ouse was under the control of the Yorkshire and District Angling Association, who for some reason put a ban on night fishing. I am sure if we could have fished through the dark hours, some of the larger chub would have abandoned their habitual caution and we might have caught some. As it was, we had no option but to make the best of the half light of dawn and dusk, which was at least better than full daylight.

As a complete contrast to the Ouse I also used to visit the Rye near Butterwick in North Yorkshire. This was a small river, marginally deeper than the Bain, and it had more character, changing from rushing shallows into deeper fast-running glides that slid into deeper pools. The Rye was, as all northern rivers, subject to sudden and unexpected spates, but we fished there often as the river had a reputation for containing some very big chub indeed. Whether this was a figment of the imagination of other anglers I could not tell, but a 4-lb chub can seem enormous to someone keen on match fishing and used to catching fish weighing only a few ounces. Perhaps a few of these mythical monster chub really existed, but we never caught sight of even one. As it was, my best Rye chub scaled $4^1/2$ lb which was at least large by Yorkshire standards.

The Derwent, wider and deeper than the Rye, but far more 'chubby' looking than the Ouse, ran deep and slow between two overgrown banks. Every swim looked as though it was a chub haven. Yet not all these perfect-looking swims appeared to suit chub. It took us many a winter, trying out swim after swim, before we discovered the better ones. Once we had found a good swim the actual catching of a chub or two was easy enough. Provided one was as quiet as a mouse and as stealthy as a Red Indian so the fish were not alarmed, they would take baits readily enough. All chub are opportunists when it comes to food and even if they are not too keen on one kind of bait, a change to another can save the day. For this reason, as well as taking bread I always take along worms as well as cubes of luncheon meat and cheese paste.

Before I lived in Norwich, I knew of the Wensum's reputation for numerous large chub and although it was a long tedious drive to get there, the effort was made worthwhile by the fishing. Certainly the chub fishing in the Wensum was as fine as any in the country and I soon discovered that by far the greatest concentration of fish favoured the stretches running by Costessey and Helsdon, two suburbs of Norwich. The average weight of fish was higher than in the Yorkshire rivers, with 4-lb specimens being quite abundant.

I had not been fishing the river for long, just the odd trip now and again when I could find the time, when I caught the fish I had been seeking for years—my first ever 5-lb chub. This blunt-headed, brass-scaled pinkish-finned and thickset fish decided to sample a fluffy piece of bread flake. As my rod bent and I felt the heavy jagging pulls on the line, I knew I had hooked a big fish. Once in the net I realised that my dreams had become reality. Weighing was just a formality to discover how much heavier than 5 lb it was: the needle finally settled on 5 lb 5 oz. What a fish!

Those reconnaisance trips were invaluable, for when I came to live in Norwich I already knew where the best swims were situated. Apart from enjoying the pike fishing for which Norfolk is justly famous, I spent much of my time tangling with the big chub in the Wensum. Some early mornings I would reach the river after a drive on treacherous ice-bound roads with thick frost on the ground and the sun shining brilliantly in a deep blue sky. Then the little river, winding through the valley, past copse and wood and hedgerow, all fluffy with hoar frost, would sparkle—a blue river, set in a dazzling white landscape like a blue ribbon around an iced cake. On those chilly mornings as the sun rose and the frost smoked, the fish lay torpid, immobile, impossible to catch.

On those days I would sit among the bankside rushes, that shone as though encrusted with diamonds, then fumble with the bait as I tried to punch it on the hook with frozen fingers. The chub, seemingly impervious to the cold, unlike other fish, would soon ease up to the bait, then opening their white-lipped mouths wide, would savour it, perhaps grateful for such easily acquired food, suck it in and then turning away downstream, they would pull the quiver tip round. Then the shivering cold was forgotten as I pressurised the chub as much as I dared, so as to prevent it plunging into some inpenetrable fastness. How deadly cold those fish felt as I removed the hooks and held them for a second or two in admiration, before slipping them back into the icy depths.

Sometimes, a howling south-westerly gale, lashing the branches, flattening the grasses and making the riverside bushes shudder violently, roared down the valley. Crouching beside the water, the quiver tip nodding in the wind making me think I had a bite, I would watch the rooks, cawing exultantly as they clawed into the air to be blown like swirling leaves across the fields. Then the surface of the normally placid, sweet-running Wensum would be transformed by foam-crested waves which slapped noisily against its banks, and the great chub stirred into activity, would hang in the current avid for food.

During one winter I caught 64 chub over 4 lb and 10 over 5 lb. A 5-lb chub, like a 2-lb roach is a target that may anglers set themselves. I count myself fortunate that I achieved such an ambition because I came to live by a river where it was possible to catch such fish. Many a skilled angler has never caught either fish of such a size; however competent an angler is, he cannot catch large fish if they do not inhabit the waters he is able to fish.

Fishing for chub is a delight not least because it is unnecessary to hump mountains of tackle down to the river, and the mobile approach, moving from swim to swim results in far more fish being caught. All that is required (apart from the rod), is a small haversack to stow the few odds and ends of tackle and a canister or two of bait. A loaf of bread can be carried in the landing net! Unencumbered, I could wander by the river fishing for some 20 minutes here a few minutes there. Always I would pre-bait a few swims with soaked mashed bread, which when thrown in at the head of the swim would sink, breaking up into smaller pieces which trundled down to where I hoped the chub would be lying. Then, returning to the first swim I had baited I would fish each swim in turn.

The chub in the Wensum liked bread, and although I caught them on other baits, I soon discovered that in winter in particular, bread in the form of flake or crust, was really the only bait I needed.

Every year there are reports of 6-lb chub being caught; any fish of that size is exceptional. Most rivers do not harbour such monsters, but some still swim in the Wye, that famous salmon river, and there are still such fish in Hampshire's Stour and Avon, now both sadly in decline. As I mention in the chapter on roach the Wensum too is not the river it was, even two decades ago. But there is hope, local anglers have formed the Norfolk Anglers' Conservation Association and they are now working in close liaison with other national conservation organisations. Together they are pressurising the authorities to deal with the evils of agricultural and sewage pollution.

Our rivers are our rightful heritage, a heritage not for anglers alone to enjoy but for all, including the generations to come. Their decline can so easily be halted if the will is there; it will take time, but I do believe that one day all our rivers will run pure. Then it can truly be said as it was by the Speaker of the House of Commons in 1655 that 'this land of ours is uncomparably furnished with pleasant rivers.'

Perch: The Buccaneering Sergeant

Many years ago there was hardly a water, however diminutive, that did not hold its stock of perch. Often the shoals comprised small fish, individuals weighing but a few ounces. Small perch are ever hungry and a couple of maggots or a wriggling worm suspended under a float would bring about their downfall with almost certain regularity. Hence their popularity with little boys, who using the crudest of home-made tackle could spend happy hours catching little perch one after the other.

Large perch, and perch can grow surprisingly large, are far more circumspect than their offspring. Once a perch (whose diet is catholic and mainly insectivorous) reaches a weight of 12 oz or so, it becomes carnivorous. From then on it commences to gain weight, rapidly eating larger and larger prey as it grows. For some reason not all perch become predatory, and those which don't and which rarely top a pound in weight tend to live longer than those which turn exclusively to a fish diet. Predatory perch can weigh 2 lb when only two or three years old. As such fish can engulf prey up to a third of their own weight, and digest such nutritious tissue to maximum advantage, their growth rate is rapid. These rapacious perch seem to have a relatively short life span, a ten-year-old fish is certainly within a few months of death. But during the brief years of its life, provided the environment is suitable and amply supplied with stocks of prey fish, a perch can reach the astounding weight of 5 lb. Even greater fish have been recorded on the Continent, and a few years ago an enormous perch of 6 lb 13 oz was netted from a Suffolk gravel pit.

Big perch, and any perch over 2 lb should be considered a fine specimen, are far from thick on the ground. A 3-lb fish is a prize few anglers ever attain, and those happy few who have landed a perch over 4 lb can truly say they have caught the fish of a lifetime.

A large perch is the only fish I know that somehow contrives to look larger than it really is. A 3-lb fish being drawn towards the landing net with spiked dorsal fin erect in indignation looks all of 4 lb. A large perch is an impressive fish, its flanks are tiger striped, its fins bristle, it is bold of eye and the whole effect is accentuated by a brilliant splash of vibrant colour, the bright orange-vermilion of their ventral fins. No fish can exude such an air of importance; a perch is by nature ebullient and supremely aggressive, and what is more can convey by its bristling presence that it strongly objects to being caught! No other fish, even that supreme predator the pike, can express its feelings so well.

Relatively few waters contain big perch, nowadays they seem to thrive best in reservoirs, particularly those that are trout fisheries. In such large expanses of water locating a small shoal of big perch is far from easy, and to make matters worse even if the perch can be found, the best method of catching them is usually prohibited. Obviously, as a big perch feeds almost exclusively on other fish, by far the best bait to catch it is a small live fish. However, small fish are very attractive to the larger trout. Fishery owners do not take kindly to their over-wintering trout being caught in the trout close season by perch fishermen. Admittedly, the trout are returned unharmed, but then other baits which are allowable such as lures, dead baits or large worms are as attractive to trout as live baits. The no-live-bait rule seems on the face of it nonsensical. Dead baits will catch perch, but they are not in the same league as live ones. However, if dead baits can be given some movement such as being spun or wobbled through the water (this method of fishing was described when pike fishing in Loch Lomond), they work quite well. So do dead baits made buoyant and twitched along the bottom.

But to catch large perch with any degree of consistency a little lively fish is by far and away the best bait. Perch will happily eat all kinds of prey; the most popular baits with anglers are small roach, rudd or gudgeon. The latter is a strong, lively little fish that lasts far longer than the others, and perch love them. If perch like gudgeon they just cannot resist a little 2–3 inch member of their own species. Strange that big perch will engulf their progeny with such gusto, but they do, and a little perch is by far the best bait for a large one. The days when hordes of little perch abounded are long gone and with small perch in short supply gudgeon are a viable alternative.

Because the perch has broad dark bars on either flank it is often endearingly called 'the sergeant' by anglers. Perhaps even more appropriate would be a buccaneering sergeant, for if ever there was a piratical fish stalking our waters on the prowl for some hapless victim, a large perch certainly lives up to such a description. Except in the depths of winter when perch stay close to the bottom in the deepest water they can find, they are active hunters. A perch shoal, acting in unison, perhaps in co-operation like a wolf pack, will chase and harry their prey with an aggressive determination that few fish, other than zander, seem to possess. Each perch will select a victim and once locked on to its target will pursue it relentlessly, grabbing and nipping at its tail fin. So a big perch will incapacitate its prey's swimming ability until it can be caught and engulfed. Then turning the fish neatly it swallows it head first.

Perch thrive in both rivers and still waters, and provided there is no shortage of suitable food will grow large even in a tiny pond. They can exist in coloured, muddy water but in such a habitat their rich colouring fades, so they appear insipid, pale and ghostlike. They rarely grow well in such an environment for they cannot see properly to hunt. It must be like trying to locate their prey in thick fog. Like all fish, perch can home in on a fish shoal by sensing their presence through the vibrations that a shoal of darting, wheeling fish emanates. But once the prey are in sight, the perch's vision takes over and the chase begins. Waters that remain clear all year

round grow the largest perch for then they can hunt without restriction. Even better are those waters near to the coast with some saline content. These are few, but both Oulton Broad near Lowestoft and Slapton Ley in Devon are slightly salty and in years gone by each of these waters has been renowned for the huge perch they contained.

Because large perch are comparatively short lived, and fish of a similar size tend to shoal together, the larger the individuals the smaller the shoal. All fish lead precarious lives; only one out of thousands ever lives to reach maturity. A shoal may contain many individuals at first but each year sees their numbers diminish. Some succumb to desire, others are eaten by pike, grebes or cormorants and as the survivors grow old they too die leaving perhaps one huge solitary fish also nearing the end of its life. This possibly 5-lb fish is the trophy that any angler would nearly sell his soul for. It is just one great fish, perhaps living in a huge reservoir.

With a normal life span of about a year the chances of catching such a fish must be almost minimal; just to find its location could take years. So the odds are stacked against the angler catching an enormous perch; there are so few that it is like seaching for a needle in a haystack. Years ago there were far more perch in our waters than can be found today. Then on one black day in 1964 a cataclysmic event occurred when disease struck and perch of all sizes began to die. First to go were the millions of perch in Windermere, it has since been estimated that 98 per cent of the perch stocks were wiped out in days. Within two years nearly every perch water in the country was affected. Like myxomatosis that decimated the wild rabbits the disease spread like wild fire, and even today the disease appears sporadically around the country. Naturally the fishery biologists did all they could to discover the nature of the epidemic, but even they were at a loss to find out why the disease struck. They concluded it was a bacterium rather than a virus, possibly one of the aeromonas bacteria. Recent research has now shown that there have been epidemics in the past. Nature is resilient, the perch survived, just, and now the species is slowly but surely re-colonising our waters. At the time Vic Bellars corresponded with fishery scientists throughout Europe, Asia and America and was surprised to discover that this disease seemed peculiar to this country. The effects are horrific: huge ulcerating sores usually affecting the fish at its posterior, bite deep to the bone. The lesions are red and eat away tissue so fast that the perch dies within hours.

But every cloud has a silver lining, and when the perch returned there were so few of them that they found more than ample food. There was no competition, the perch could eat their fill and consequently grew as never before. Soon the angling press began to report the capture of 4-lb and even 5-lb perch. Today, even if not as numerous as before, the perch population is stable; it would have been a tragedy if such a noble and handsome fish had been lost to us.

If small perch are suicidal, always avid for worms, large perch are exactly the opposite. The larger the perch the more wary it becomes. Being aggressive by nature it will take a bait readily enough, but if it encounters any tackle resistance it will eject the bait instantly. Ninety-nine per cent of big perch act so, but there is always the unexplainable exception. Now and again a perch succumbs to a large bait, complete with hooks attached to wire designed to catch pike. Vic tells me that once an enormous perch picked up a whole herring that was lying on the bottom when he too was pike fishing. That particular fish cared not a jot for resistance. Somehow it managed to grab the herring while avoiding the hooks. But in spite of Vic striking, thinking a pike had taken the bait and then reeling in all of 50 yards of line, that perch hung on as if it was a point of honour not to let go. It only did so a split second before it would have found itself enmeshed in the landing net.

The proliferation of Specimen Groups coincided with the advent of perch disease so quite naturally no one gave a thought to perch, simply because there were hardly any left. And while the specialist groups refined and developed very sophisticated tackle rigs in order to outwit their favourite species, to this day very few anglers know how to set about catching large perch. This state of affairs is sure to change however, and just recently a number of anglers from Kent, a county well endowed with perch, have formed the Perch Fishers. I expect to see within the next few years, innovative tackle rigs, new techniques, and a greater understanding of the habits of perch emanating from this new organisation. If they are as successful as the carp anglers, and there is no further large-scale epidemic of perch disease, who can guess how large some of the perch caught in the future might be?

When I was a teenager I used to fish for perch with my father. Perch disease was unknown, and we used to fish in a complex of three lakes just two miles from home. These waters were situated in a pleasant parkland setting known as Greaseborough Dam; they are now called Wentworth Fisheries.

Small and medium-sized perch are easy enough to catch, hence their popularity with not only small boys but adult anglers as well. Catching

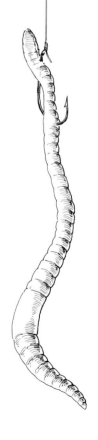

these perch was fun, and a pleasant respite from fishing for other species which were rather more difficult. The tackle we used to bring about the downfall of the 'sergeants' was hardly more refined than the dangled worm technique invariably employed by small boys. We dangled worms too, suspending them under a brightly-tipped float so they wriggled enticingly at a depth of five or six feet, at mid-depth in water some twelve feet deep. As the perch were so accommodating we did not have to wait long before one of our floats would dip, then slide away visible for a second or so before sinking deep. Sometimes, both our rods would be bent at the same time, tips flagging in response to the aggressive tugs of the hump-backed perch had suddenly discovered that some worms were not quite what they seemed. I still remember those halcyon days, gazing in admiration at these moderate but vividly striped sergeants. When released, their fins erect like a yacht under full sail, they would dive down into the depths with a sinuous twist that rippled the length of their bodies and with a disdainful flick of the tail.

On one day when our floats never stayed on the surface for long, and we were happily making inroads into the perch shoals, my float sank yet again. This was no bustling little fish. The rod hooped, and a series of powerful thumps and surges made me yield line hurriedly. After what seemed an age I got into the landing net what appeared to be an immense perch. It was by far the biggest I had ever seen; a prize so unexpected that I could hardly believe my good fortune. That perch dwarfed its fellows, and after the scales had registered $2\frac{1}{4}$ lb my whole nonchalant attitude to perch fishing changed for ever. If such a fish could be caught at Greaseborough Dam what other even larger fish were there for the catching? Alas, I never had the chance to discover the truth for shortly after, the shoals were wiped out by disease. I had to forgo all the plans I had been formulating, but I never forgot, and over the succeeding years my thoughts often turned to big perch and the best way to catch them.

A few years later I used to fly fish for trout at Chew Valley lakes. Blagdon and Chew were long established and famous fisheries—lovely lakes gently enfolded by soft West Country hills nestling at the foot of the Mendips. Although fishing for trout, just occasionally as I slowly retrieved my fly, inching it through the water deep down I would feel a savage tug. Unlike the trout which when hooked would run far and fast, often leaping clear of the water scattering rainbow-coloured droplets that spattered the surface, these fish stayed deep, thumping away at the rod tip. Then, as I played the fish nearer, I would glimpse the large-finned and bared flanks of a hump-backed hog of a perch. These were wonderful brightly-coloured fish and nearly all of them topped the 3-lb mark.

But others, and in particular the dedicated game fishermen, did not share my delight. Once an angler fishing not far away landed a gem of a perch, well over 4 lb. Expressing his disgust, I watched as he kicked that magnificent fish up the bank and let it die, flapping weakly as it slowly suffocated. Such behaviour apart from being inhumane was inexcusable; I was sickened. Attitudes have changed now, and as more and more coarse anglers enjoy trout fishing their concern for their quarry has percolated through the ranks of the game fishermen until there can hardly be any such bigots left.

While these great perch lived at Chew the disease raged on elsewhere and it was only recently that I have been able to go fishing with the sole intention of trying to land big perch. All trout waters, including the large reservoirs, soon became colonised by other species. For years coarse anglers have sought permission to fish during the trout fishing close season. This has always been opposed by the trout anglers, but at last those controlling such waters have come to realise that they would gain further revenue if they opened their waters for coarse fishing. So more and more trout waters can be fished for other species and one of the first to open was Ardleigh Reservoir near Colchester. Ardleigh can be reached quite easily from Norwich, so Derrick Amies and I decided to have a day or two on the water pike fishing. On one of our earlier visits I watched while another angler, also pike fishing, landed a fine 3-lb perch that had fancied his large 6-oz pike bait. Immediately my yearning to be able to fish for large perch was rekindled and from then on I planned and schemed with only one thought in mind: big perch. The following weekend we went afloat with a bucket full of lively little gudgeon, light rods, and reel spools filled with 3-lb breaking strain line.

Vic Bellars has made a speciality of devising resistance-free tackle rigs specifically for perch fishing. One of these consists of a small balsa wood float finished in black and green camouflage. The float is fitted with a revolving eye at the top and another eye is set in the base. To this bottom eye a 4 to 5-foot long length of line is secured which terminates in an Arlesley bomb. The reel line is threaded through the eye at the top of the float, through a small bead and knotted to a swivel. The hook length some 12 to 18 inches long is joined to the swivel. When cast out the bomb holds bottom and the float rises to the full length of the bomb link holding the bait up well away from the bottom. When a gudgeon is presented on this rig it tries to swim down to the bottom but as it dives the buoyancy of the float restricts this activity. But the gudgeon keeps trying, and by so doing sends out a continuous series of vibrations which are likely to be sensed by any large perch in the vicinity. When a perch takes the bait it can run off taking line without encountering any resistance whatsoever. Vic designed this rig for bank fishing, tensioning line to the bomb so that the float was angled towards the rod helping to mitigate the problem of the gudgeon tangling the hook length with the bomb link.

However well a boat is anchored it is bound to swing a little, so in order to fish with rig efficiently, Derrick and I had to hold our rods so as to keep the line tensioned to the bomb. The gudgeon could be felt tugging away until a firmer tap on the rod tip showed a perch had taken it. The reel bale arm was opened as quickly as possible so that the perch could swim away freely. Because the gudgeon were just lip-hooked the strike could not be made at once; normally we waited for a few seconds watching line trickling off the spool and feeding through the rod rings before setting the hook. It was always exciting during those few moments as line poured away, to ponder if a really huge fish had taken the bait after all. Perch always run off with baits be it fish or worm, acting like a chicken that has found a tasty tit-bit and runs off to some obscure corner, so that other chickens cannot steal its prize.

Ardleigh produced some wonderful perch; I landed eighteen smaller fish of about 1 lb in one session, and once I caught one at 3-lb 4-oz, one at 3 lb 2 oz and one at 2 lb 9 oz. This was a red letter day. Another angler caught one of 4 lb 4 oz and as all of us have only begun to scratch the surface one is tempted to surmise that even larger fish are there for the catching. It will not be easy now that live baits have been banned, and we shall have to try out dead bait techniques. If these are not too successful we'll have to devise new ways of presenting dead baits that are attractive to the larger fish. We have yet to use large lobworms, and even a perch normally used to feeding on other fish would, I think, hardly pass by such an easy meal. One problem we encountered at Ardleigh were the pike. They too liked our gudgeon but 3-lb line is no match for such a powerful fish. Unless hooked away from the teeth, the line was immediately severed as though drawn across a razor blade.

I would dearly love to catch a monster perch and that ambition has never died since I caught my 2-lb fish at Greaseborough. Although I have never seen one I have my own mental image of what a 5-lb perch must look like. A 5-lb perch, now wouldn't that be just something?

Of all sports, fishing can lead to frustration, despair. tranquillity and elation in equal measure. However skilful or experienced there is always more to learn, so much so that even after a lifetime, the angling jigsaw puzzle only hints at the completed picture.

The driving force within an angler, the force that drives him out in gale and rain and snow, is inexplicable to others. However articulate a fisherman may be he is at a loss for words with which to describe his feelings. All I can say is that I find beauty, unfathomable mystery, elation and sorrow, and above all profound intellectual fulfilment when I am fishing. For millennia man was a hunter. Now that he has no need to hunt in order to survive, it does not mean that his inherent instinct to hunt has been lost. It is only suppressed, buried deep in his unconscious, papered over by the veneer of civilization. It is when the veneer cracks and the instinct surfaces that some men become anglers.

As I come to write the last two chapters of this book I realise with perhaps some sense of shock that I have been a fisherman for half the normal life span. Yet there is so much still to do, so much still unlearned. My mind reaches out, thinking of all the fish still to catch; the huge Danubian Wels, a giant catfish that can grow to over 200 lb in Eastern European waters; the great muskies, the North American pike that fight like tigers; the gargantuan Nile perch of African lakes; the wild mahseer that press against the cold Himalayan currents that torrent down Indian rivers; the chinook salmon that lie deep in Lake Michigan and the huge pike that beckon from Holland and the Baltic Sea.

There will never be time, but I can plan and dream and hope. For surely hope lies deep in every angler's heart as he sits peacefully beside some tranquil lake, apart from other men, attuned to nature and the ways of fish.

A 3lb 4-oz perch from Ardleigh Reservoir near Colchester.

Roach: The Silver, Red-Finned Fish of Rivers and Lakes

Until carp fishing mania spread like an epidemic through the ranks of coarse anglers, the roach had been by far the most popular fish. Yet if a poll was conducted today, roach might even now top the list—not because of its size, because small ones are ridiculously easy to catch, nor even for its beauty—but because the larger ones are fewer in number and more difficult to tempt. To catch a large roach with consistency the angler must be skilled at watercraft and acquire expert knowledge of the various waters, both still and running, so he can locate the larger fish among the millions of smaller ones. He must also be adept at using refined techniques and delicate tackle.

There is hardly a tiny pond, little stream, canal, river, lake or gravel pit that does not harbour roach. There are roach in Loch Lomond, in the finest and most exclusive trout rivers such as the Itchen and Test whilst in that mighty salmon river, the Tweed, roach glide the current rubbing shoulders with their more aristocratic neighbours the trout and salmon. The roach is a prolific species, a fish at home in any unpolluted water and like small perch, small roach have helped to instil into small boys a love of angling, so that they grow up to become keen fishermen all their lives.

To some, the pike is the freshwater shark, the bream ever on the move graze the bottom like sheep, dace, darting silver, flit in the current as active as the swallows that sweep low over their heads feeding on the emerging flies, the olives and sedges. But the gentle, tranquil roach, gliding over the gravelly bed of a stream, slipping through the waving fronds of water plants is the queen of rivers. Large roach are majestic fish, and since it is every angler's ambition to catch a two pounder, a 3-lb fish is a rarity indeed and must be considered the fish of a lifetime.

Roach swim in shoals. I've called them gentle because they threaten no other species, they pursue their peaceful precarious lives unobtrusively in cool waters, and perhaps because of their abundance, are the natural prey of other predatory species that share their environment. Pike, perch, chub and eels, as well as the more recently introduced zander, harry the roach shoals. So do the great crested grebes and the heron. Such heavy continuous predation takes its toll, but the roach have had to survive such dangers from time immemorial; they are a fecund species adept at survival.

The back of a roach is a cold electric blue, that fades into silver irridescent flanks that then merge into the pearly white of its underside. Like the red eye of the tench which is complementary to its olive green body, so the bright orange iris of a roach's eye complements its bright blue-scaled back. A roach's fins, tissue-like in their transparent delicacy are tinged with orange-brown. A large roach wet and glistening as it is taken from the water is beautiful to behold.

Happily there are still millions of roach in our waters, though roach in the rivers are in decline. At first their numbers dwindled due to industrial pollution. In spite of the recent efforts to mitigate this evil, agricultural pollution in the form of pesticides and leaching of excess chemicals from fertilisers, still causes immense damage to river life. While many mature fish are able to cope with such changes in water quality the young fry in their first year of life do not seem able to tolerate such conditions.

Nowadays, far fewer waters contain really large roach, but even when they were relatively prolific many an angler never caught one. Yet such is the unpredictability inherent in the sport of angling, and that surely is the challenge that makes the sport so fascinating. I caught my first big roach when I was just eleven years old. It was a wonderful, unbelievable fish of 2 lb 3 oz. Few small boys have been so lucky and to add to my excitement I won a competition run by the *Star* supplement for the best fish caught that week. As winner I received the then princely sum of £5. It was a fortune; I spent it on fishing tackle.

That memorable fish came from the little river Bain which flows south through the heart of Lincolnshire, and passes through Horncastle and Coningsby before it becomes lost in the Witham. In the Sixties the Bain had a reputation for its fine roach fishing. Two-pound fish were not uncommon, and it was believed that even larger fish, perhaps reaching the magic weight of three pounds existed, but they were of course extremely scarce.

In summer the Bain was as slow moving as a canal, but in winter the water was allowed free passage in anticipation of the floods which occurred at regular intervals. This completely changed the river's character. It flowed faster with deeper pools and eddies on the bends. As a youngster I was privileged to accompany my dad and his friends and other

Winter roach, both just under 2lb.

Two 3-lb rudd from a Norfolk lake.

Rotherham Club members. Until then I had fished for much smaller roach in the canals, dams and reservoirs close to home.

Every Sunday I joined the coach load of anglers, often in the chill dark winter mornings at 5 am. The journey took some two and a half hours to reach our destination, the popular stretch of river near Coningsby. We fished all day, then at dusk the coach would pick us up for the journey home. I was always tired out but would not have missed those Sundays for all the world. To begin with the coach was usually full but as the years passed the number of anglers diminished somewhat, though always enough turned out to make the trips worthwhile.

Many of the stalwarts worked in the steel and coal industries, and the one day a week spent in the rural peace of lowland Lincolnshire was a necessary antidote to the noise, grime and physical labour that they had to endure for six days out of seven.

Even while so young I came to realise that if I was going to catch big fish I would need the drive, enthusiasm and the urge to travel to good fishing waters. If I remained near home I would only be fishing for smaller fish and struggling to catch even them. Perhaps that huge roach fired my enthusiasm, but today I am still prepared to travel hundreds of miles for good fishing.

As has happened on so many roach rivers the numbers of large fish have inexorably declined, being replaced by the ubiquitous chub. This thrusting omnivorous species, with a marked predatory tendency colonised the better roach swims, competing for food and generally ousting the roach from their accustomed haunts.

There had always been a few chub in the Bain; they seemed to favour the deeper holes sheltered by overhanging trees while the roach preferred to station themselves in the water no more than three or four feet deep, ahead of the chub lies. As well as roach I used to fish for chub too, and the best I caught from the little river was a bronze broad-shouldered fish of 4 lb 2 oz.

So every winter Sunday, rain or shine I joined my father and his helpful angling friends, keen to learn as much as I could by watching and fishing with them. We fished very simply, ledgering maggots downstream on the river bed, using fine lines and tiny hooks. In order to hold the bait on the bottom the line was passed through a pierced bullet or the eye of any Arlesley bomb. We tightened the line to the bait then watched the rod tip for bites. Usually there was a hardly discernible nod, a gentle pluck before we swept the rod upstream to set the hook. On such gossamer tackle, a big roach can fight hard; we had to play such fish with extra care and it was often a minute or two before we glimpsed our quarry flashing silver beneath the surface.

Naturally, having caught such a fine roach whilst still so young, and larger than any roach caught by some of the experienced anglers who were my mentors, I was keen to catch an even bigger one. So with each trip my enthusiasm grew, as did my angling techniques. I fished hard and moved to the Witham which was quite unlike the little Bain except in its higher reaches. Lower down the Witham was wide and deep, a typical fenland drain set between high flood-retaining banks. Here, as well as roach were bream, great shoals of them beloved by the match anglers. My horizons widened, I found new challenges. After years of fishing the Bain, the Witham and other fenland waters our band of anglers decided to try pastures new. A trip was planned to take us far north to the border country, to that legendary river that flowed into the North Sea at Berwick, the Tweed. Even those who have scant knowledge of angling must know that the Tweed is one of the finest salmon rivers in the land. So my mining and steel working friends were off to fish a famous river where wealthy men sporting deerstalkers paid a fortune to rent a salmon beat.

Of the fine roach these gentlemen paid little heed, except to lodge complaints and request their removal from the river. In spite of regular netting, the roach survived, so roach fishermen were welcomed in the hope they would kill the fish they caught, or at least find another home for them. This was a strange attitude, for once a salmon has entered fresh water it ceases to feed, intent on only driving onward to reach the spawning beds in order to perpetuate its species. I suppose the young salmon parr dropping down river had to compete for much the same food as the roach, as would the trout which were abundant. There was no shortage of food for either species, but there are still just a few game anglers remaining who consider any fish other than salmon and trout to be vermin. Happily these attitudes are changing; there will always be some roach in the Tweed.

Fishermen who fish this stony, boulder-strewn rushing river, startled when a great salmon leaps from the water by their float, can enjoy some of the best roach fishing in the islands. While some large roach in tiny isolated shoals shelter in the deep pools and eddies where the current slackens, the average size is below the 2-lb mark. But the attraction of the Tweed for roach anglers lies in the quality of specimen fish, many exceeding a pound in weight that swim in the river. A 1-lb roach may not seem much of a prize to the layman, but to catch such a fish in any

The author sits poised for action on a summer's day.

Derrick Amies and a 6^1/$_2$-lb tench from Johnson's Lake.

numbers is roach fishing at its best. These were not the ultra-cautious fish that I had been accustomed to, but bold biting roach that came to the net one after the other, fighting hard, bending the rod and utilising the current by pressing their broad flanks against the flow of water.

Because the bed of a river such as the Tweed is boulder strewn, we could not ledger but used a float, letting the maggots trot down the swim just clear of the bottom, much as I had first fished for barble. The float itself, specially designed for fishing moving water was called a stick. Stick floats are buoyant by the coloured tip—the tapered lower section is made of denser material so the float when correctly shotted rides the current vertically. When trotting a bait down river it should move with the flow in as natural a manner as possible, it should not be dragged along, but be carried at exactly the same speed as the current at the depth at which it is presented. If by subtle variations in the pattern of shots below the float the bait can be persuaded to move ahead of the float, and not be dragged or pulled sideways, a fish will accept it as a natural item of food borne along by the flow.

In order to achieve this very necessary bait presentation the shots on the line below the float are evenly distributed and graduated from the largest near the float to the smallest nearer the bait. It may sound rather complicated but the different ways in which a float may be shotted to suit water conditions whether it be used in still or running water is not difficult to master, yet I still encounter anglers who consider themselves experienced, who do not fully comprehend the most efficient way to shot a float.

After a long coach journey through the night I set eyes on the magnificent Tweed. Like all northern game rivers, it flows fast and turbulent in the wide shallow stretches. The water piles up, foaming against protruding boulders and boils over those just below the surface. But in the quieter deeper pools where the salmon rest before driving on toward the headwaters, the flow is more gentle. Here the roach shoals congregate, waiting for food to be washed down to them.

I wandered the bank looking for just such a pool, I found one where the river turned, checked the depth and decided that was where I would fish. In no time a handful or two of maggots were scattered into the head of the pool so that they would be carried by the current downstream, sinking even lower until they neared the bottom in the heart of the pool itself.

I swung the float out, watched it work upright and as the flow carried it along paid out line from the reel so that the float's progress was

unchecked. All the time my eyes were glued to the brightly-coloured tip, starkly visible against the dark mysterious surface of the pool. It slid under and stayed down indicating a confident, positive bite. This was not the finicky tentative dip of a float that I was used to indicating a bite from a well-educated roach! On every occasion I had a bite the float slid away and every time I lifted the rod in response I hooked a fish. And what roach they were. As pristine and brightly coloured as any that I ever caught. They were large too, many well over a pound in weight, real specimens that any roach angler would have been proud to have caught. Just a couple would have made the day but as fast as I trotted the bait downstream it was intercepted. Not one fish I caught weighed less than half a pound; it was roach fishing such as I had never dreamed of.

I could hardly drag myself away from the banks of that noble river. What a day! The weather, the scenery and the fishing were perfect. I lost count of the time, of the numbers of large roach that seemed to come to the landing net in an endless stream. Who knows how many roach I really caught or indeed what weight of fish? Perhaps a very conservative estimate would be 60 lb.

Not that it mattered, what was far more important was that I had enjoyed superlative roach fishing that few anglers ever experience. Much as I longed to visit the Tweed again to find other pools, and walk miles of bank in seeking them, the distance from home made this impossible, as did of course the expense.

Roach in lakes and those in rivers need different techniques to catch them. After many years mainly concentrating on the Bain, the Witham and other rivers, I realised that if I was to become more knowledgeable concerning the habits of roach and more expert at catching them, I should come to terms with the greater difficulties of catching large roach from still waters. Any angler worth his salt can walk the river bank and discover swims that should hold a roach shoal, but in the featureless expanses of lakes or gravel pits, a purely visual exploration is well nigh useless. Nevertheless, to me such problems only act as a spur, and the greater the difficulties the greater the challenge.

It was most fortunate that just when I was turning such problems over in my mind I read a report in one of the angling papers that some fine roach had been caught from a twenty-acre lake near Worksop, called Clumber Park. This was an amazing stroke of fortune for this was only twenty-five miles away, near enough for me to fish virtually whenever I wished. Clumber Park is comparatively shallow but the water deepens at

Four early-season chub from a Norfolk river, all taken on floating crust.

An 11lb 6-oz bream from a Norfolk lake.

one end near Hardwick village. It is a timeless place, the lake nestles in ancestral parkland and is so well wooded as to be reminiscent of Sherwood Forest. Whenever I fished at Clumber I always had time to enjoy its ancient beauty.

The lake not only contained large roach, but shoals of bream forever patrolling the bottom were abundant. A few tench and the odd big pike lurked beneath its rippling surface. While popular with match anglers fishing through the midday hours, Clumber Park lake did not seem to attract those who just enjoy a day's fishing. It was from the reports of those who did that I learned that a large roach was sometimes caught.

By now a member of the Hallamshire Specimen Group and owner of an ancient van, I decided that with Clumber Park so near I would plan a campaign with the sole object of catching some large stillwater roach. Having had to travel far to find good roach fishing in the past it was good that I had found a fine roach water virtually on my doorstep.

I was lucky too, that September—always a good fishing month—lay just ahead. I intended to fish as much as possible in that month and to continue right through the winter until the season closed in the following March.

I had now convinced myself that Clumber Lake would produce some very large roach if I was prepared to fish as often as possible and put in the effort without which I could not succeed. I became doubly sure when I learnt that some three or four specimen group anglers had also been fishing the lake. Such anglers would not bother with a water that was not capable of producing large fish. My confidence grew.

When fishing an unknown water it is rare to catch the larger fish by finding a comfortable pitch on the bank and fishing hopefully. There are many chores, and by far the most important is to discover the structures of the lake bed. Only by knowing intimately the underwater terrain can the probable location of the bigger fish be determined. Not a little time has to be spent surveying the water, then when promising areas have been pinpointed they can be fished in turn. Only by such means can the best swims be discovered. By steering clear of the more popular swims I discovered a quieter length of bank opposite, the bottom features of which I felt sure would attract the larger roach. This side of the lake was heavily wooded. Some two hundred and fifty yards across the water lay a peninsula that jutted out into the lake, but I discounted this at first, because the car park was close by and such a swim was sure to be popular.

I selected two other places, cut back the minimum of vegetation so I could cast easily, then constructed two small platforms in each swim by cutting into the step bank. Sheltered by shrubbery I could fish in either place, virtually unnoticed except by the most observant. There were no signs that others had fished this particular bank which was near the dam. This was a bonus for any roach frequenting the area would not have been fished before.

The water was quite shallow near the bank, in fact I had to wade out a few yards in order to cast my baits into the deeper water. The areas I wanted to fish lay some sixty to seventy yards out. I soon learnt that the roach always remained far out in the lake and never seemed to venture close inshore. It also became apparent that the more delicate the tackle the more bites ensued. I had to use 3-lb breaking strain line and a gossamer hook length of 1.7 lb and at times had to go even lighter, right down to 1.1 lb.

A 3lb 4-oz rudd from an Oxfordshire pit.

To cast such distances I used a swimfeeder full to the brim with maggots. On one rod I chose a type with open ends which was blocked to hold the maggots inside with dampened breadcrumbs. As this sank down to the bottom, the breadcrumbs activated by water tended to burst out, releasing the maggots almost at once. The feeder on my second rod had permanently closed ends, except that the cap on one end could be removed so that it could be filled, then replaced. Once this type reached the bottom the maggots could only escape via the holes, so that for some time a steady trickle of maggots was released to crawl around the maggots on the hook. Apart from giving the necessary weight for casting, the feeders concentrated the bait close by the hook. It was the only feasible method to lay groundbait accurately at such a range. Such a tight concentration of bait naturally attracted any passing roach shoal, and as the fish finned over the loose offerings their gyrations formed currents and vortices. These would cause the maggots to be lifted off the bottom, rising and swirling so they would be eagerly snapped up. The agitated water would affect the hook bait in the same way which would then behave exactly like the groundbait so that it was likely to be taken with confidence.

All big roach in whatever water, seem to feed best when the skies are overcast, and if a wind ripples the surface, blowing towards the angler, conditions could not be more perfect. But however bright the day, when light values are low, at dawn or dusk, the larger fish seem to feed in earnest.

My first two evening trips to Clumber coincided with a strong westerly wind and nearly full cloud cover. But the wind which had been blowing from the same quarter for some time had caused a strong undertow flowing away from the bank. This caused my bite indication bobbins to rise, and I had to pinch up to six heavy shots on their retaining lines to hold them down.

Usually the first bites materialised after the baits had been in the water for some twenty minutes. Sometimes the bobbin climbed steadily upward, but now and again they dropped down. In either case an immediate response was required and the rod had to be swept upward and backwards. Nylon line stretches under tension and the more line in the water, the greater is the degree of stretch. Because of this the strike was cushioned—the line was acting as a shock absorber so that the force was not quite enough to cause the frail hook length to break, yet sufficient to set the tiny hook.

As autumn passed and winter set in I became so familiar with the roachs' feeding times that I could predict the event to within ten minutes. Knowing their habits I would arrive at the lake with my rods already tackled up so as to cast out my baits just before I expected the fish to commence feeding. Night fishing was prohibited and roach feed well for the first two hours of darkness. But the friendly bailiff turned a blind eye, and I was often allowed to fish on into the darkness undisturbed. Usually the night-time fishing was so good that even before my arrival I was certain, if there's any certainty in angling, that I would land one of those specimen roach.

As the winter progressed and far fewer anglers braved the elements I tried fishing from the peninsula. Well out in the middle of the lake from the point was a channel of deeper water, this was at least eighty yards away and to reach such a distance I had to use more powerful carp rods and more heavily weighted feeders. The shock of casting so heavy a weight would have parted my fine 3-lb line, so I used a shock leader. This technique borrowed from sea anglers who need to cast heavy weights when distance casting from the beach, made it possible to cast the eighty yards with ease. A shock leader consists of a length of strong line, just a few yards, knotted to my weaker one and long enough to allow a few turns on the reel spool. Now I could compress the more powerful rod with the heavier swim feeder so as to project it the long distance I needed. It was interesting to note that when I arrived at the lake in the late afternoon, an hour or so before darkness fell, any anglers who had been fishing were packing up their gear, just before the larger fish were likely to start feeding. They must have thought I was leaving it rather late!

It did not seem to matter how unpleasant the weather or how cold it became—those obliging roach did not seem to care. More than once I fished with ice at the margins, the water in the main body of the lake still unfrozen but looking dead and lifeless. In spite of the penetrating cold which seemed to increase in intensity as the light faded the fish continued to feed and I was able to predict to the minute when to expect the bobbin to rise indicating a positive bite. Once braving a snowstorm which completely blotted out the landscape, I became engulfed in an horizonless capsule of swirling white. During that blizzard I landed a magnificent blue-backed roach of 2 lb 7 oz not to mention others between 1 and 2 lb. Some of my friends also caught similar fish in much the same bitterly cold weather; we seemed to be proving all the books I had read on roach fishing to be sliding misleading.

Sometimes it was so arctic that the line froze to the rod rings making bite indication by bobbin useless, but then ignoring the resistance those hardy fish tugged the rod tip and we still managed to hook them.

I had a red letter day landing three roach over 2 lb and during one winter netted one hundred fish over 1 lb, included in that total were sixteen fish over 2 lb and a superb specimen of just 2 oz under 3 lb.

In spite of such successes I experimented with other techniques and other baits. In particular, those baits which had proved excellent elsewhere, such as a pinch of flake from a new white loaf, little red worms such as can be found in their hundreds in any compost heap, and casters, the chrysalis stage of the metamorphosis of the maggot to the fly. I tried these alone and in combination, cocktails in angling terms, worm and casters, bread and maggots but none proved more deadly than just maggots alone. I even tried long-range float fishing while it was still light enough to see the float tip, but unless the water surface was calm, it was difficult and tiring on the eyes to see the float among the ripples. So always I returned to fishing with my swimfeeders and maggots and this method proved to be by far the most consistent.

When I left Rotherham to live in Norfolk, Clumber Lake was so far away I had to find another water. The choice between yet another lake or a river was all too easy. The Wensum, where I was to enjoy the finest barbel fishing had a reputation for harbouring huge roach, even over the 3-lb mark. Sadly I arrived too late, halcyon years were over and only a few of the large roach remained, now old and nearing the end of their lives. All our rivers have declined, at first due to industrial pollution, now the pesticides. The water abstraction and the leaching from the land of nitrogenous fertilizers, as well as the discharge of sewage effluent, have altered the water quality for the worse. These evils and indiscriminate weedcutting at the wrong time of the year when tiny fish need cover to survive their first precious months of life, have decimated the fish fry. No doubt a few live to reach maturity but not enough for the steady replacement of the older fish as they die from natural causes. This unhappy state of affairs had already materialised when I went to Norfolk. However, there were a few widely dispersed shoals of huge roach patrolling in the Wensum which I hoped to be able to locate and then fish for.

As with the Bain and so many other rivers the hardy, ebullient chub had encroached on the roach swims. Chub were not indigenous to the Wensum but had been stocked in the river by the water authority. They thrived, and were particularly abundant in the lower stretches near Norwich. I like chub fishing. and I love trying to outwit the larger ones, so I fished for these chub hoping to come across a roach swim in my wanderings. The bite from a chub and a large roach affects the sensitive quivertip spliced into the rod end in different ways. Luckily the Wensum roach take kindly to bread flake, a favourite chub bait of mine, so I would note any swim where roach were located. Once I had a few roach bites I later returned to that swim with rather lighter tackle and a much smaller hook. From Norwich upstream to Swanton Morley odd roach survived, but my favourite stretches were at Hellesdon and Costessy where the river, although so close to the city suburbs, is quite unspoilt. Here the river winds past woods and copses and is bordered by green water meadows. There are intriguing deep holes, where the flow slackens to form eddies close to the undercut bank on a bend. While such swims were beloved by barbel and chub the roach seemed to station themselves upstream of these features in a glide of medium depth.

In summer the prolific weed growth in the Wensum made roach fishing difficult but after the first frosts, the weeds died back rapidly and the first floods washed away the rotting stems. Then, with most swims clear of weed it was time to seek the large roach.

As at Clumber Lake, the fish fed best as the light faded and dusk crept along the valley, and continued to do so for an hour or two of total darkness. But unlike at Clumber hard frost and bitter weather affected the Wensum roach to such a degree that they became torpid and ceased to feed entirely.

I did eventually land some fine roach but was saddened that it was likely to be many years before such fish would be replaced by the natural order of things.

As a roach river, the Wensum today is hardly worth fishing, anglers are now only interested in its barbel and chub, but it is still a wonderful river and unless some calamity occurs such as further heavy pollution it will, albeit slowly, recover in the years to come. Already the pressures from conservation organisations like the Friends of the Earth, and the anglers themselves have encouraged the authorities to make a start in the eradication and treatment of the more insidious pollutions. After years of pressure the drainage engineers have finally agreed not to cut the water weeds just when the roach are spawning, and to allow some weed to remain as shelter for the emerging fry. If the agricultural pollution can also be controlled the Wensum can recover.

Then the roach will return to establish themselves throughout the whole river and shoals of lovely gentle fish will hover over the gravel beds once again to brush the water weed against their silver flanks. The queen of the rivers will once more swim in her ancestral home, the quiet and peaceful Wensum.

Pike: The Supreme Predator

The rotund coot, its sombre grey-black feathers only relieved by startling white forehead shield and ruby eyes, swam purposefully from the sheltering stand of Norfolk reeds towards a bed of water plants nearby. Here in the bottom silt of the shallow Broad was its favourite food; succulent green fronds that thrust upwards to the light and mingled with the surface ripples. With winter in the offing, the coot began to fill its crop, vigorously pulling at the weed stems. Like all wild creatures heavy autumnal feeding is instinctive, for when the iron frosts iced the Broad inches thick, food would be unobtainable. Only the thick layer of fat accumulated during this period of gluttony would sustain life through the lean mid-winter.

This Broad, hardly changed through the centuries, was set deep in the wild flat land of eastern Norfolk. Grey water lying under a wide sweep of sky rippled against the acres of ochre-coloured reeds, whose feathery seed-heads bent ever resilient to the Siberian winds that can roar across this open land, and churn the sheltered waters into a froth of spume-laden waves.

As the coot moved from one patch of weeds to another, its long-lobed toes thrust against the water. Pressure waves radiated from the centre of disturbance symmetrically, as ripples form when a stone is dropped on the surface of a pond.

Some yards away, creamy white underside pressed gently on the bottom sediment, lay a huge shovel-nosed log of a fish. She too, obeying Nature's urging, was keen to eat her fill. This pike, deep of girth and broad of back, lay in ambush, immobile. Her olive flanks, dappled yellow, blended in camouflaged perfection with the gently swaying weed. Little changed genetically, if at all, from her ancient forebears this superb predator shifted her position restlessly. In the mists of pre-history other even greater pike had stalked the vast meres, of which this Broad was but a shadow, a medieval peat bed reverted to primeval fen. This we know, for one carcase turned to stone survived, a fossil left for us to wonder at.

The coot's gyrations released yet another pattern of pressure waves, and

just before they dispersed to be lost among the ripples, a hardly perceptible current caressed the pike's flank. The sensitive nerve cells ranged along the lateral line were activated. The large dorsal and ventral fins set well back immediately in front of the great sweep of tail, quivered. The pectoral fins positioned just behind the slowly pulsating gills fanned minutely, and with a lazy push of her tail the pike re-orientated herself until her crocodile head aligned exactly with the unseen disturbance. The long lean fish inched steadily forward; her sonar had locked on target. Two yellow-ringed eyes set forward in the skull for binocular vision searched the circle of light above. The coot, still tugging at the weed shoots, lifted its head every few seconds instinctively, for from the moment it had struggled exhausted from the egg, its survival depended on constant vigilance. The pike gliding relentlessly forward, scanned the light circle. Suddenly a dark hazy form materialised, faded then reappeared distorted by refraction, and further diffused by the clusters of silvery air bubbles trapped in soft plumage.

Tensing, the pike launched herself upwards, fast as an arrow leaves the bow, ramming a surging bow wave before her. In that same split second the coot thrust its wings down and using the surface for leverage, flung itself up and sideways, legs trailing in a smother of spray that fell and mingled with the swirling vortex caused by the pike's lunging turn. Skittering across the Broad, the coot plunged into a tangle of reeds, its plaintive, staccato cries echoed by other hidden coots sheltering deep among the stems. With a sinuous thrust of its torpedo-shaped body, the pike swept aside the weeds and again lay still, resting on the bottom of the Broad while the fog of displaced silt settled slowly around her. That September evening with the sun low over the western horizon, my son Neil and I moored our boat on the Broad, with the bowline hitched around a bunch of reed stems and a mudweight lowered over the stern to prevent the boat yawing excessively.

It had been a frustrating day. Still working for British Rail, I had spent the off-duty hours serving in my tackle shop. I had been hoping to close early, but customers, for once unwelcome, kept arriving—with my new business taking so much of my free time, I could rarely go fishing and that day I had planned to spend at least an hour or two on the Broad. At last I was free to lock up and, it being much later than I had expected, we had a hectic drive to the dyke where the boat was kept. Racing against time and the inevitable onset of twilight, we flung rather than stowed the tackle aboard which was to be sorted out as we navigated the river. The outboard running at full throttle drove us onward, the propeller forming an impressive wake astern that widening, slapped the reed margins, then rebounded to meet the waves reflected from the opposite shore to form a criss-cross pattern of ripples that only died away some hundred yards astern. Reaching the entrance to the Broad, I cut the motor then rowed quietly towards the great reed bed at the eastern side. I poled the last few feet, pushing the bow into the reeds so that Neil could secure the mooring line.

Two light powerful rods, constructed of carbon fibre and thin at the tips, were quickly made ready. The baits—herrings, smelt and roach—lay in the cool bag, fresh and ready for use. The large landing net was assembled. At last we could soon start fishing.

We had noticed as we entered the Broad that groups of wildfowl dotted the surface. Coots were abundant. Mallard were upending or busily paddling from one weed bed to another. A great crested grebe still attended by a pair of fully-fledged young, was diving repeatedly. The two young grebes, although perfectly capable of hunting the silver roach shoals themselves, rushed towards their parent every time she surfaced, hoping for an easy meal. Cheeping vociferously, they spattered across the water, wings beating, legs and feet flailing sending a spray of water droplets falling behind them.

Busy with our tackle, I had for a few minutes ceased taking an interest in all this fascinating activity, when Neil said 'Dad, have you noticed the birds have gone?' I looked up, the main expanse of water was devoid of wildfowl. Only a few remained close by the reeds and one coot, not thirty yards away, was still actively feeding.

As I watched, the water erupted by the coot, the sound of the splash was loud, startling. As the turmoil of spray and swirling water subsided the coot flew headlong deep into the reedbed. Such a commotion could mean only one thing to an angler, some large fish had betrayed its location. Experienced angler though I was, my pulse still quickened at such a sight; the hunter's instinct breaking through the veneer of civilisation. With single-minded intent and using all the guile at my command I set out to capture the quarry that had unwittingly shown itself. Hands trembling a little I attached the two small needle-sharp treble hooks to one of the herrings. With the bait suspended beneath a scarlet-tipped, cigar-shaped float I cast the bait close by the widening ripples. The herring blue-backed, silver-white with crimson eyes and gills sank slowly, enticingly, and lay on its side at the bottom of the Broad. The float, weighted so that it would

Two pike, 23lb 12 oz and 22lb 8 oz, from the Broads.

float vertically, bobbed and wobbled for a second, then stilled, the scarlet top appearing twice its length due to its reflection in the placid surface.

The trap was set.

As the herring splashed down, the great pike felt the vibration. The pressure waves brushed her flank. A cloud of silt rose behind her tail as she turned unerringly, pointing her head towards the disturbance. Sliding forward, she sensed the herring's aroma carried in the oil slick that had begun to permeate the water. The hunter was hunting again, but this time unknown to her, the roles were reversed.

She took the herring gently, gripping it crosswise in her jaws, and clamping down hard she crushed to kill. This was instinctive even though the herring was dead. Then with gills flared open, so that the filaments shone crimson, the pike ejected the bait—so fast that it would have been hardly discernible to an onlooker—and re-engulfed the herring, this time head first, before she moved away ready to swallow. She became aware of the restriction of her movement too late, her head was pulled sideways so powerfully that she keeled over on to one flank. As with all wild creatures in mortal danger the pike sought refuge in flight. Righting herself, flexing her long muscular body and raising a great cloud of mud as her tail lashed from side to side, she surged away.

As I picked up the second rod, the float dipped and sank beneath the surface, I quickly lobbed the bait near to the reeds on my right and handed the rod to Neil. I quickly picked up the first rod as line was peeling steadily from the reel spool. Pointing the rod tip to follow the line, I turned the reel handle which automatically engaged the bale arm. Reeling in quickly until the line tautened I swept the rod upward and a little to one side, to set the hooks. The first powerful unstoppable run stripped off yards of line, then hurling itself upwards the pike cleared the water, its long olive-green body twisting, as with mouth agape it shook its huge head from side to side and crashed back on to the surface. She surfaced once more and charged across the Broad, half her body length clear, tail-walking and churning the water into foam. Plunging down she suddenly changed course and ran towards a weedbed. The taut line cut a V-shaped wake and still line had to be given as the shocks transmitted through the rod to my hand, warned me that an extra energetic lunge could break the line. Should this occur it would result in a double tragedy: the loss of a great fish, but worse, a fish with hooks embedded in the jaw, which unless the pike could rid itself of them could impair its capacity to feed. Perhaps this was the make or break point in the contest. I had to apply as much pressure on the fish as I dared,

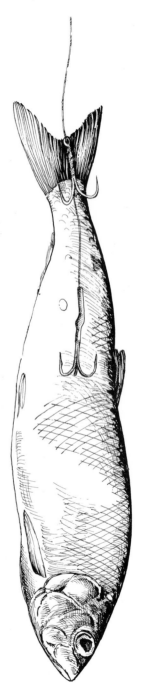

judging exactly the amount of force I should exert to prevent her reaching the sanctuary of the weeds without the line parting. It's during moments such as these that for a fleeting second you wonder if you tied the knot securing the line to the swivel of the flexible wire leader correctly.

Feet short of the weeds the pike turned, then surged away on the surface, her body twisting from side to side, sinuous and eel-like, pushing a steep bow wave ahead of her. Once more she shook her head but the hooks, deep in gristle, held firm.

Fighting to the limits of her power had slowed her speed, sapped her stamina. The expenditure of oxygen in the blood feeding the muscles was so great that they became starved and the build up of acid so impaired their efficiency that the great fish slowed; her rushes became weaker and the huge tail now swept from side to side lackadaisically. She was led grudgingly and reluctantly towards the boat. Neil, eyes wide with wonder, extended the net frame below the surface, and waited. The pike now floated on her side, the long green-dappled flanks shining wet, and the huge orange striped and mottled tail, stilled. With fully bent rod I guided her head over the net, pulling her up towards the junction of the outspread arms, then easing the pressure her head sank and that great body was enveloped in the soft meshes.

The enormous sense of relief I felt lasted hardly a second or two when Neil shouted 'The other float's gone.'

I grabbed the rod, telling Neil to keep the pike and net in the water, Once again I swept the rod up vertically until I was forced to ease the pressure and let the fish swim away with increasing speed.

This time the pike reached the weeds and powered underneath the surface mat deep among the stems. In such a situation, if the rod is held high the line can collect heavy, clogging weed, so I plunged the rod tip deep into the water exerting a heavy relentless pressure on the fish and keeping the line clear of the tangled weed mass at the surface. For some time, but possibly only seconds, the honours were even. The pike could not push further into the sheltering weed and I could not pull her out. The stalemate continued, then suddenly the water heaved and the pike gathering speed cleared the weed fronds and endeavoured to put as much distance as possible between herself and her unseen adversary. She fought hard, careering off in a series of blistering runs, testing my tackle almost to breaking point. But, inevitably the fish tired and after one last short, head-shaking spurt, she allowed herself to be led quiescent and docile to the side of the boat.

A 46^1/$_2$-inch Broads pike weighing 30 lb 1 oz, taken on small livebait.

Summer rudd fishing on a Norfolk lake.

But the battle was far from over, with one large fish already in the net the only way to secure this pike was to manhandle it into the boat. The technique is difficult especially with so big a fish; fingers must be slipped under the chin and inserted into the junction of the gill covers. Then with a firm steady lift the fish can be eased over the gunwhale. What made this procedure even more hazardous was that the pike had been hooked by only one set of treble hooks. The other treble hung free outside the mouth. A flying treble is dangerous if the fish twists or thrashes as the hooks can become deeply buried into a hand or arm. The risk had to be taken, there was no alternative. Praying the fish wouldn't kick, I leant down, found the gill clefts first time and heaved her into the boat where she lay on the soft carpet underlay lining the floorboards; if she thrashed now she could do herself little harm.

The state of the boat was chaotic: one huge pike inboard and the other still in the net over the side. Both had to be unhooked and their weights ascertained.

The fish in the boat was quickly unhooked then laid in the dampened weighing sling which had already been hung on the dial scales so that they could be zeroed and her weight recorded exactly. Under the weight of the fish the needle spun round the dial, steadied, quivered and registered 25 lb 3 oz. Quickly this big fish was transferred to the black keepsack and lowered over the side. Fish lie quietly in darkness and so can regain their strength prior to release. We weighed the first fish likewise, she too was a 'twenty', the needle indicating 23$\frac{1}{4}$ lb. Neil and I 'sacked' this pike as well, and during the time we had been dealing with both fish an event occurred which is rarely witnessed. The calm water of the Broad was shattered as one pike after another began to feed. It seemed as if every pike in the water was striking at the surface. Loud splashes, enormous vortexing swirls, bow waves scything across the surface and occasionally a shower of fish leaping from the water indicated a pike in pursuit of some helpless shoal. Perhaps an apt description of the pikes' behaviour would be that they were all engaged in a feeding frenzy. They rampaged through the water herding and harrying the shoals of roach and bream, each pike selecting a victim then taking it with a lunging turn that left a great swirl of eddying water at the centre of a widening circle of ripples.

With such a magnificent spectacle holding our attention it was difficult to drag ourselves back to the work in hand, but with the light fading, time was running out. We had at least to restore some sense of order in the boat before fishing once more. As quickly as possible two more baits were cast out, and even more quickly the floats were pulled below the surface. This time Neil had to take charge of one rod. I saw him strike, noted the impressively bending rod, and set the hooks into another powerful fish which forced me to yield yard after yard of line.

There is always the chance with two fish being played at the same time that the lines can cross and a tangle occur, possibly leading to the loss of one or even both fish.

The pike I had hooked was fighting hard, so calling out to Neil that he should do his best to coax his fish as far away from mine as he could, I concentrated on mastering a fish that fought even harder than the two fish recovering in the sacks.

In such a situation, all sense of time is lost. In what seemed like a quarter of an hour, but in reality can only have been three or four minutes, I netted a pike that appeared to be even larger than the others—and so it proved; it weighed in at $27^1/_2$ lb of muscle-packed predator. This fish was long and lean, its stomach wall slack. Had it fed well during the preceding days it could have weighed a magical thirty pounds. Neil's pike, just over half the size, was unhooked and gently lowered over the side so it could slide away into obscurity.

Unbelievably, both our new baits were swiftly taken. Niel played and landed a $14^1/_2$ pounder and mine yet again topped 20 lb by 1 lb 4 oz.

Still the pike in the Broad fed and still we caught them. After a 17-lb fish was netted and released, we felt we could not continue. We were both mentally and physically exhausted.

We released the two smaller 'twenties', photographed the largest and with these returned too, we rested awhile as darkness fell and the reeds turned blue-black against the last orange glow of the western sky. Pike were still striking, swirling and bow-waving as in a daze I rowed slowly towards the river. Occasionally resting on the oars I mused, a kaleidoscope of thoughts racing through my mind.

Clear of the Broad I started the outboard, the chattering engine sounded discordant, alien in the wilderness of reed and fen.

The riverbank slid past dark and mysterious, the first stars gleamed faintly and the breeze blew chill. Reaching the dyke we secured the boat and humped the gear to the car. As we drove along through the village and turned on to the Norwich road Neil and I spoke little, each lost in his own thoughts. I wondered how many anglers had had the fortune to catch four 20-lb pike in as many minutes. Even today I have met only one or two who have witnessed such an explosion of rampaging pike. The memory will remain sharp and clear for Neil and me for the rest of our days.

At dawn the first skeins of wildfowl patterned the lightening sky: the mallard came first, then widgeon, recent arrivals from their breeding grounds in northern tundra and one sprig of teal that, sweeping low over the Broad, rocketed upward at some imagined danger. The duck set their wings, falling and whiffling down like swirling autumn leaves, levelled out, then planed over the water. With tail feathers spread wide and webbed feet thrust forward to act as airbrakes, they settled. Then dispersing to feed, they were joined by some coots that left the reeds and swam, heads jerking, towards their chosen larders.

The sun now clear of the horizon, glazed the reed tops and the light flooding over the Broad began to illuminate the twilight underwater world of weedbed and age-old sediment.

Here, the pike sulked the night away, her stomach still empty, flaccidly pressed against the silt.

The red-finned roach, each deep of body with orange eyes complementing blue-scaled backs, drifted along the edge of the weedbed jungle and fed desultorily. As one roach upended to suck in a morsel of food its life was instantly extinguished. Held first by needle sharp teeth, it was crushed with vice-like power then engulfed. The roach shoal reacted instantaneously, flashed away and upward, packed tightly for protection each fish echoing exactly the movements of the others. The shoal's synchronised behaviour, was an instinctive reaction to danger developed in the species through millennia of evolution. But soon the shoal slowed and turned, individual members drifted apart and once more fed independently and seemingly unconcerned.

The pike, her hunger satisfied, eased her body beneath a canopy of weed and lay quiescent.

Century after century long before man penetrated this windswept fen the same drama had been enacted: predator and prey, each playing their age-old roles in order to maintain Nature's precarious balance.

The surface of the Broad turned a deep ultramarine blue, two tones deeper than the blue of the sky. Sunlit ripples sparkled as the morning breeze strengthened and sighed among the reed stems. The water warmed as the sun climbed even higher and one great pike, now replete, lay comatose. The supreme predator had at last, fed.